The Sixties and Seventies

The Golden Age
Of Magazine Illustration

To Céline

Gilles de Bure

The Sixties and Seventies

The Golden Age
Of Magazine Illustration

EDITIONS DU COLLECTIONNEUR

© 1997 Editions du Collectionneur
13, rue du Cherche-Midi
75006 Paris
Editorial Director: Dorothée Walliser
Translated by Lois Grjebine
Production: Gilles Tarral and Emmanuelle Demont
Colour separation: Colourscan
Printed and bound in Italy by Milanostampa

ISBN: 2-909450-42-2

Forward

Magazine illustration is something very special and specific. It is quite distinct from what is commonly known as press illustration, that is to say, political cartoons, caricatures or humorous drawings. It is also different from comic strips, advertisements or posters, or graphics for cultural events.

Somewhere on the frontier between the plastic arts and graphic art, magazine illustration has as much to do with journalism and sociology as with visual expression.

All the works presented here come under the heading of magazine illustrations. There are, however, a few exceptions, for the author made brief incursions into the fields of book publishing and posters; certain illustrators have made such major contributions there that their work cannot be left out. In a similar vein, it is difficult to confine certain very original creators like Ungerer, Topor, André François, Folon or Roman Cieslewicz solely to the field of magazine illustration. The most patent exception here is Guy Peellaert, who never worked for magazines, yet whose illustrations of music during this period so neatly fit the editorial thrust of this book.

Clearly we make no claim to be exhaustive. Quite the contrary. We present here only a selection of events and situations which made a profound impact on society during the Sixties and Seventies and that were admirably told in images by a handful of gifted artists.

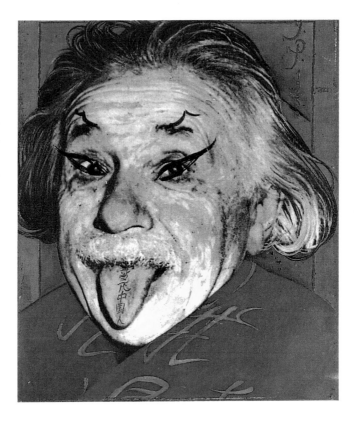

Gabriel Pascalini
Lui, no. 194, March 1980.
"Yi-King, la Chine en avant toute !".
Article on China's atom bomb.

The Great Image-Makers

Reasonableness was certainly not what characterized the Sixties and Seventies. Rather, these were years of revolt and utopian dreams, of struggle, hope and disillusionments, of unexpected and unpredicatble events.

History was in the making. History with a captial H, as well as a more modest, "lower case" history made up of daily observations and feelings. The latter nonetheless made profound changes in attitudes and behaviour for years to come.

Was it possible to capture these notations, these vibrations, these fleeting sensations? There came to the fore a generation of artists or illustrators (depending on the epithet one prefers to use to describe these image-makers), who chose to commit their observations to the pages of magazines, preferably monthlies.

This generation of image-makers was born just before, during or immediately after World War II. They experienced first-hand these eventful decades, realizing that they were banner years, marked by ideological commitments, as well as by political battles, both verbal and physical. While others took to the streets, they took up their pencils. Their drawings are a reflection of the questioning and questing, the unflagging enthusiams, fads and madcap schemes of the times. Together, they constitute lively, living memoirs of the Sixties and Seventies.

There are many different ways to write history. Images are the most instantaneous mode of notation, for they can pull together and communicate news that is as diverse as it is abundant, fleeting and kaleidoscopic. The act of bringing together the most significant images of daily life is like fitting all the pieces of a puzzle. Once completed, it affords a view of a highly complex reality.

Magazine illustration can be an incisive tool for deciphering what is taking place. In the right hands, it can be a vigorous, efficacious way to present political, economic, social and cultural events, while highlighting their mythological and at times mystifying aspects.

For nearly twenty years, magazine illustrators filled an area that was temporarily vacant. Television news coverage was still in its infancy and was only just beginning to exact its toll on photo reportage. As television cameras could broadcast on the screen events as they were actually taking place, photos eventually became too static for public taste. At this point in time, however, photo reportage did not as yet look outdated, but it was certainly less essential than before.

In short, photo coverage was no longer what it used to be, and television was not yet what it was to become.

For magazine publishers, this meant that editors had to aim to reproduce not the first images they could lay their hands on, but the best. And that is how photo reportage came to leave more than enough room for what could be called illustration-journalism. In one image, illustrators could not only transmit information but could also tell a story about it. They could analyze and interpret an event, provide commentary and even give it a special twist.

This technical, professional explanation, however, is not sufficient to explain the blossoming of magazine illustration

Miriam Wosk
Milton Glaser
Charlie White III
Andresjz Dudzinski
James McMullan

during years that were marked by successive social upheavals and a gradual evolution of mind-sets and behaviour.

Upheavals and gradual changes in attitude are never easy to render, but they were manna from heaven for editorial illustrators, whose commitment was equal to their talent. Sharing traits with plastic and graphic artists as well as with reporters and political commentators, magazine illustrators forged an art form that was no doubt limited and ephemeral but also incredibly powerful and meaningful.

Each of these illustrators honed his own set of tools, developing his techniques and specific talents to forge a style that was visually easy to identify. It is impossible to mistake Davis for Le Saux, Ungerer for Lagarrigue, Glaser for Topor, or Cieslewicz for Chwast. Each in his own way constructed a visual "vocabulary" to express both the sociological truths of the times and their symbolic value.

Addicted to news reports, personally dedicated to certain new values, under the sway of new messages, and bound of course by the nature of their assignment, illustrators were quite naturally inclined to denounce the hidden sway

of reigning ideologies, to lay bare the flaws of consumerism in an affluent society and to announce the new manners and modes of the day.

The magazine illustrations of the period give a good idea of the rise of utopian dreams and of the newfound faith in the future. Youth was convinced of the need to wipe the slate clean. They were determined to make majors changes in everyday life, as they gleefully blasted myths and shibboleths, made fun of their elders, and denounced hypocritical behaviour. What the young were looking for was a new sense of identity. They wanted those who had kept silent to speak up. Editorial illustrators reflected these changes.

Lashing out at the past, speaking up for the present and staking a claim for the future, they claimed the right to be at once militant and humorous, profound and frivolous, refined and vulgar, jubilant and despairing. They handled these extremes with mastery, voracity, ingenuity and perversity. As the reader moves from chapter to chapter through this book, he will find a heady mixture of anger and humour, whether the drawings deal with politics or social upheavals, people's attitudes or their behaviour.

Paris and New York were without doubt the capitals of this flowering. By comparison, London, Los Angeles, Warsaw, Tokyo, Milan and Berlin were mere outposts. Why Paris and New York? No doubt because the high concentration of magazines in both places offered immense opportunities. Another likely reason was that publishers' attitudes were not as yet perverted by sales charts. Beliefs had not hardened into certitudes. Publications, whether weeklies or monthlies, were not considered merely as vehicles for advertising.

Thanks to the exceptional atmosphere that reigned during this scant twenty-year period, magazines became a curious mixture of art and sociology. In the United States, the most outstanding vehicle for illustrations was the New Yorker, a veritable institution, known for its brilliant cover illustrations. Other leaders in the field were McCall's, Life, Holiday and Audience, subsequently supplanted by Esquire, Playboy, Show and Sports Illustrated, and in another register, by Ramparts and Evergreen. The trend was reinforced by the launching of Rolling Stone, New York Magazine, Ms. and New West.

In Paris, the two pioneering publications were Elle (with its lonely hearts column) and the men's magazine Lui (starting in 1963). Equally notable were Playboy (in 1972), Twenty, Kitsch with its small run-off, and Actuel, which introduced Crumb to the French public. Last but not least, there was the short-lived Paris-Hebdo, launched by publishing magnate Jean-Louis Servan-Schreiber with Jean-François Fogel as editor-in-chief and Jean Lagarrigue as art director. In 1981, in the space of three short months and twelve issues, Lagarrigue published some of the most outstanding illustrations of the time. Other influential European press organs were Twen in Germany, Szpilky in Poland, and in Great Britain, Punch, the Sunday Times, Time Out and Nova.

Memories of the hardships of the postwar period grew dim as the economy prospered, and the time would soon be ripe for revolt and utopian dreams. In the aftermath of the giant conflict that shook the world between 1939 and 1945, the biggest priority was to heal wounds, to repair and to rebuild. Much of Europe and Asia was devastated, whereas the United States, despite its preponderant role in World War II, had not suffered physical damage at home. On the contrary, the huge war effort had created a dynamic of its own. The United States had increased its industrial capacity and was producing more every day. Its international power grew commensurately.

Starting in the Fifties, the stage was set; the USA would set the pace for the rest of the world. Its postwar economic edge was to ensure American hegemony over the rest of the world for decades to come. From New York to Los Angeles, in Boston, Atlanta, Chicago and Detroit, Americans were forging our modern Western society.

Off the production lines of General Motors came automobiles for the masses. William Levitt built suburban mass-produced houses for America's middle class (but off bounds for blacks). The towns were such a hit that they became known as Levitt-towns, heralding the heyday of suburban developments and New Towns. In 1953, Eugene Ferkauf built the first shopping center on the outskirts of New York, which preceded out-sized supermarkets. Dick and Mac, the McDonald brothers, were making a fortune in California and were starting out to conquer the world with their hamburgers.

Television was going through growing pains, reaching its majority with the election of John Fitzgerald Kennedy, who was incomparably more telegenic than his rival Richard Nixon. In 1955, biologist Gregory Pincus developed the first contraceptive pill, which was finally approved and put on the market in 1960; it marked the beginning of sexual freedom and women's liberation.

The nuclear race was hotting up, and the conquest of space became a major stake in the Cold War. For ten

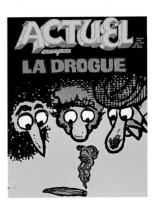

Charlie White III
Milton Glaser
Barbara Nessim
Gilbert Shelton
Milton Glaser

years, from 1959 to 1969, space became the main battleground for the two super-powers, who by turn gained the upper hand. In January 1959, Lunik made its first flight. On April 12, 1961, Gagarin became the first cosmonaut to man a space flight, and on March 18, 1965, Leonov left his capsule Voskhod II for ten minutes, taking the first walk in space. The USA countered six years later: Edwin White stayed outside Gemini IV for twenty minutes. The Soviet Union got the upper hand again in January 1966, when Luna IX landed on the moon, but the United States countered with the space probe Surveyor 1. It won the space race when Neil Armstrong stepped outside his capsule at 3.56 am on July 21, 1969. As he took his first step on the moon, Armstrong made that historic comment: "A small step for me, a giant step for mankind".

The Cold War took on many different forms: Castro took power in Cuba in 1959. The Soviet satellite, the German Democratic Republic, raised the Berlin Wall, physically separating the former German capital from the West. In his famous "Ich bin ein Berliner" speech on June 26, 1963, President Kennedy made a commitment to keep West Berlin firmly anchored to the West.

Roland Topor

George Hardie

André François

Jean-Michel Folon

The great hopes of the postwar generation faded with the Cold War and the balance of terror. During the same period, Great Britain and France learned the painful lessons of decolonization in India, Indochina and Algeria. One direct result of the Algerian dilemma was to bring De Gaulle back to power.

The youth of this generation, coming of age in a world with so few ideals to offer, reacted by creating its own heroes: Elvis Presley in 1954, Marlon Brando with "On the Waterfront" and James Dean in "Rebel Without A Cause", the revolutionary leader Che Guevara, and Marilyn Monroe, a gorgeous sex symbol, yet touching and vulnerable. A counter-culture took shape. The Beatniks, with Jack Kerouac as standard-bearer; the "Nouvelle Vague" (New Wave) with film-makers François Truffaut, Claude Chabrol and Jean-Luc Godard; the "Nouveau Realisme" (New Realism) with painter Pierre Restany; the "Nouveau Roman" (New Novel) with Alain Robbe-Grillet; and last but not least Free Jazz with Ornette Coleman, Eric Dolphy and Cecil Taylor.

Novelty, freedom, the road, the first hints of youthful revolt gave rise to some unexpected and even startling encounters. In Paris, the first issue of the literary review Tel Quel came out in 1960, led by Philippe Sollers and Jean-Edern Hallier. About that time the French were also offered the first issue of Hara Kiri, dubbed the "dumb and mean" magazine by its promoters; the team included Cavana and Choron, Gébé and Reiser, Willem and Wolinski.

Films, too, heralded the end of an era and the beginning of another. Some were nostalgic, others dark and disturbing: "Jules and Jim" and "Le Feu Follet" in France; "The Misfits" and "West Side Story" in the United States; and "Tom Jones" in Great Britain. Rockers were cropping up everywhere, known as teddy-boys in England and "blouson noirs" ("black jackets") in France.

It was in this pernicious atmosphere, in a world torn asunder by the Cold War and colonial wars, by an increasingly avid consumer society and the space race, by disenchantment with a worn-out system of values and explosive new social situations, that this generation of magazine illustrators came of age.

Their early production coincided with the end of the Fifties and the early Sixties; their art was really flourishing by 1963-1964. Those were the years when Eric Losfeld published the "first" cartoon strip for adults, Jean-Claude Forest's "Barbarella", which Roger Vadim brought to the screen three years later, with Jane Fonda starring in the title

Paul Davis
Esquire, 1965.
"28 people who count".

Paul Davis
Look Magazine, 1970.
"Changing symbols".

role as the female instigator of protest. Spearheaded by the works of Claude Levi-Strauss, structuralism was in full bloom. Its literary ramifications were explored by Roland Barthes and Jacques Derrida. Jacques Lacan founded the Freudian school in France, and Louis Althusser provided a new interpretation of Marx. Michel Foucault was preparing to publish "Les Mots et Les Choses", while in Brussels and Paris a number of writers sharpened their pencils: Guy Debord ("La Société du Spectacle"), Raoul Vaneigem ("Traité du Savoir-vivre à l'Usage des Jeunes Générations"), Georges Perec ("Les Choses") and Jean Baudrillard ("Le Système des Objets"). These questionings and criticisms were taken up in visual form by the happenings of the Fluxus group and the audacious Pop artists. In New York in the late Fifties, the Push Pin Studios were taking shape around Milton Glaser and Seymour Chwast. They attracted followers for many years to come. Among them were some of the most talented illustrators of the time: Paul Davis, James McMullan, Jerome Snyder, Sam Antupit, John Alcorn, Vincent Ceci and Barry Zaid. They put all types of media to use to display their vision, eclecticism and mastery, from the press and books to posters and ads.

This was not the case in Paris. Instead, rather than forming a professional association, a number of friends simply banded together. There was a sense of complicity rather than a common ideology or editorial line.

At one time or another, Jean Lagarrigue, Alain Le Saux, Philippe Corentin, Gabriel Pascalini, Jean-Claude Castelli, Jean-Paul Goude and Jean Allesandri, among others, all belonged to this loosely knit group. Their overriding concern was to make the commissions they had been given tie in with their own personal convictions. The best illustration, they believed, was like a good joke: it had to be short, to the point and have a great punch line. The aim was to use the least to get the most, to take a single idea and squeeze the most out of it. It could take as many as thirty or forty drawings to succeed in wringing the most succinct symbol out of that idea.

A number of illustrators, like Le Saux, Corentin and at times Quarez, had a penchant for cartoons; others, like Lagarrigue, Pascalini, Goude and Castelli, stuck to realism. But for each and every one of them, and in all their sketches, one can find the same determination to head straight for essentials, to round up everything —the idea, the com

mentary and its ramifications— in a single image. The illustrator had to follow the message where it took him and he had to show personal commitment. This was a very French "high-wire act". The initiators were no doubt André François with his slightly out-of-phase but nonetheless scathing humour (see page 120) and Tomi Ungerer. One could add Roland Topor, who

XDR

relentlessly denounced the Vietnam war and social inequalities (pages 20, 33, 34, 35…). They were certainly the most iconoclastic and irrepresible of the image-makers. Among American illustrators, the only ones who could compare were Paul Davis and later, when Women's Lib was under full steam, Hedda Johnson, Barbara Nessim and Miriam Wosk, as can be seen in the chapter entitled "Women On the March" on page 58. The precursor in the United States was, of course, Norman Rockwell, who was always irreproachably politically correct.

As for lineage, the visual influences are very evident. These editorial illustrators were the direct descendants of Gustave Doré and Magritte, Steinberg and Morandi, Hopper and Pop Art, Dubout and Chaval, Savignac and Hergé. They were cousins of satirists Crumb, Reiser and David Levine.

None of this could have happened, however, if it had not been for the enthusiasm and dedication of certain art directors who sincerely believed that their newspapers and magazines had to have as strong a visual editorial line as a written one.

There were people like Malcolm Maveridge for Punch and Harry Peccinotti for Nova in Great Britain; in Germany, Heinz Edelmann for Twen; in the United States, Jim Geraghty and Lee Lorenz at the New Yorker, Robert Weaver for Sports Illustrated, and Walter Bernard and Milton Glaser for New York Magazine. Without doubt, the crucible in the USA was Esquire, which had a succession of great art directors: Henry Wolfe, George Lois, Robert Benton (who left publishing for the film industry, writing Arthur Penn's "Bonnie and Clyde" and

15

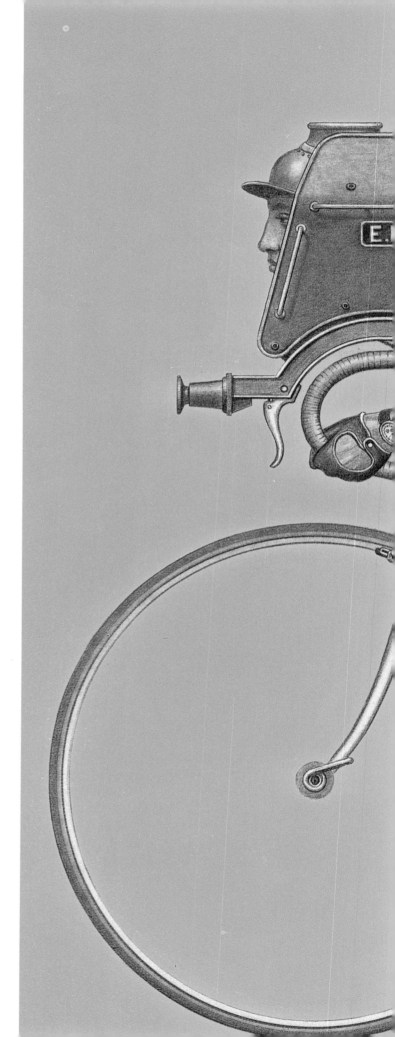

Jean-Claude Castelli
Lui, no. 78,
July 1970.
"Le chouchou
de Bruxelles",
on Belgian
cycling
champion
Eddy Merckx.

directing "Kramer Vs. Kramer"), Sam Antupit and two young Frenchmen dropped down in the middle of Manhattan, Jean Lagarrigue (from 1968 to 1970) and Jean-Paul Goude (from 1968 to 1973).

In France, leading lights were at Elle magazine (Peter Knapp, Jean-Louis Besson, Jean-Louis Faure and Roman Ciselewicz) and the ubiquitous Jean Lagarrigue at the short-lived Paris-Hebdo. But the main thrust was to be found in the Filipacchi group, at the new men's magazine Lui, founded in 1963. Art director Régis Pagniez created an original style that lasted a good fifteen years, from 1963 to 1978. The style was perpetuated with the French version of Playboy, another Filipacchi production, that began in 1972.

On both sides of the Atlantic, the stage was set between 1957 and 1963, with the play reaching its climax between 1968 and 1970. But by 1978, the actors had lost their punch, and the show finally closed.

The world of images was not solely the preserve of magazines. Things were also changing in the field of satirical publications as well as animated cartoons. Walt Disney passed away in 1966, and two years later Heinz Edelmann did the drawings for a feature-length animated cartoon dedicated to the Beatles, called "Yellow Submarine". In 1969, the illustrator Wolinski launched Charlie with Cabu, Reiser, Bretecher and Pichart. The following year saw the end of Hara Kiri, closed down by the government for having announced the demise of General De Gaulle in his home town of Colombey with the irreverent title: "Tragedy Strikes Colombey Dancehall: One Dead."

During these years, the issues addressed by magazine illustrators mirrored current events: the rise of minorities and recognition of minority rights; anger against tyranny and totalitarian regimes; irreverent treatment of the establishment; the new depiction of women and their specific identity, as the feminist movement helped women move from submission to liberation. Concomitantly, illustrators pinpointed "macho" behaviour in its old and new forms and took a close look at the effects of rising antagonisms over sexuality, the couple and the family.

They also reflected the rising importance of psychoanalysis, which was making the general public aware of repression, psychoses, and the growing feeling that everyday life could be hell and that paradise could be gained artificially. The harmful effects of modern life were becoming clearer: ecology movements were springing up, and new humanitarian action groups were getting off the ground. Music seemed to take on even more importance than in the past; sales were soaring, and records were reaching new segments of the population. It was not enough for singers and musicians to be on the hit parade; they had to be turned into star-myths, which echoed the new obsession with youth. For European youth, of course, anything that had to do with America was at once attractive, repulsive and fascinating. The American way of life became the model to copy, despite the belief of left-wingers that capitalism was exploitative and ought to be denounced.

These were two very short decades, for the great flamboyant outburst lasted for only fifteen years, from 1963 to 1978. By 1978, the old left-wing belief in "pie in the sky" and tomorrows better than yesterdays was being seriously

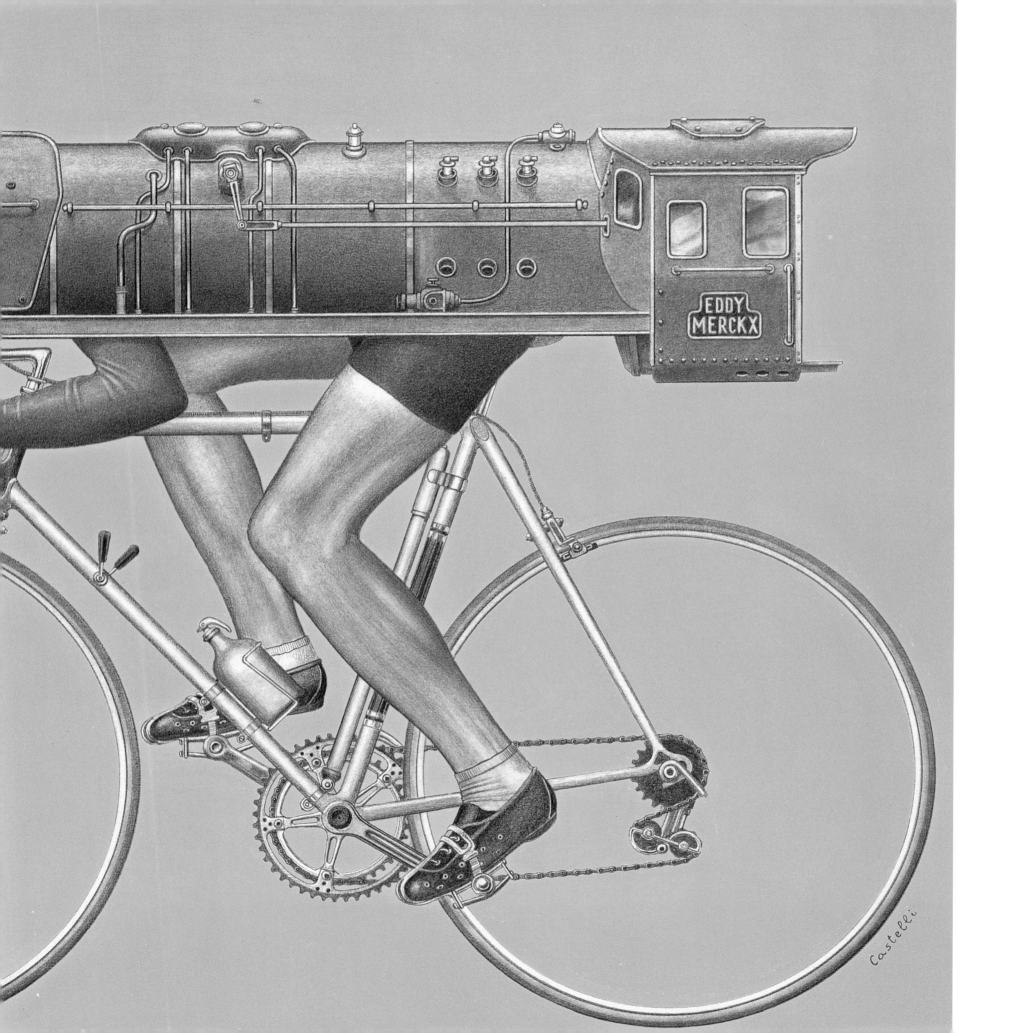

Roman Cieslewicz
Cover of
Opus no. 4,
1968.

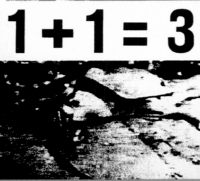

Roman Cieslewicz
Cover of
Kamikaze no. 2,
1991.

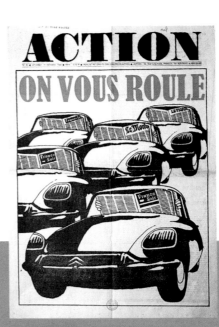

Michel Quarez
Cover of Action,
June 1968.

Alain Le Saux
Lui, no. 187,
August 1979.
"URSS… mal
léchée", or the
effects of vodka in
the USSR.

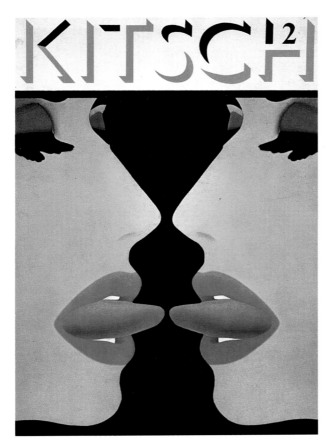

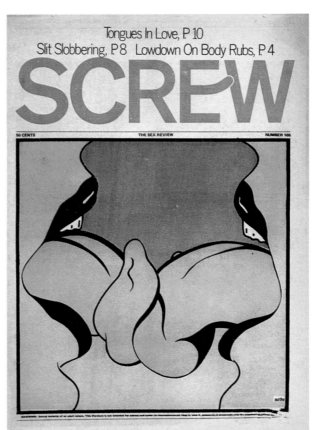

put in question. The profile of the coming decade was looming on the horizon. In France, the trend could not be halted, even by so iconoclastic a group as Bazooka (comprised of Lulu Larsen, Kiki Picasso, Loulou Picasso, Bananar and Olivia Clavel), who sometimes dubbed themselves the "Electric Clito". It was they who produced an insert called "Un Regard Moderne" (roughly, "A Modern Look") in the left-wing daily Libération. They also did the credits for a television show called Chorus, led by Antoine de Caunes. In other words, dailies and even television were taking over from magazines, which in turn were reverting to photography and an occasional humorous drawing.

The Eighties were to mark the end of utopias, the end of political and personal commitments. Society was heading towards consensus and overriding egotism. The "Me First" generation was going to win out over the romantic lyricism of the Seventies, finally crushing its hopes and dreams.

Among the more acerbic illustrators, like Ungerer, Cieslewicz, Davis, Le Saux, Quarez and Castelli, the shape of things to come was already fairly obvious. Behind the optimism, there was lucidity and despair.

The train of ideas and events led to a curious succession of decades. It was as if the Sixties with its themes of "autonomy, identity and being different" followed directly in the wake of Claude Levy-Strauss's "Primitive Thinking" ; as if the Seventies, marked by the theme of sex, drugs and rock 'n roll, were following on Jerry Rubin's "Do It" ; as if the Eighties were following on Guy Debord's "show-biz society" with its infatuation with "business, spangles and night clubbing" ; and as if the Nineties, marked by "AIDS, unemployment and rave" had come down in a direct line from Brett Easton Ellis's "Less Than Zero".

No matter what one chooses to call them, a generation of artists/illustrators came of age during the Sixties and Seventies, showing outstanding gifts for graphic inventiveness and a commitment that was as rigorous as it was humorous. Like meteors, they left in their wake ephemeral traces of exceptional brilliance.

Tomi Ungerer
"Black Power/White Power".
Poster, 1967.

20

The Fight For Autonomy and Identity

Indochina was heating up. The fight for independence from colonial powers came hard on World War II. It was soon to be echoed by another type of struggle, this time for personal freedom. Individual demands were for more autonomy, for the right to one's own identity, for the right to affirm differences.

Around the world, fires were being lit that to this day are not completely extinguished. On January 1, 1959, in a great coup that was to hold out hope and serve as an example for other revolutionaries was the coming to power in Havana of Fidel Castro and his "barbudos". In 1961, only a few months after the assassination of Patrice Lumumba, who was raised to the rank of mythical figure, Frantz Fanon published "The Damned of the Earth" which quickly became a kind of international handbook of the world's convulsions.

The struggle of the colonized against colonial powers and man's fight for man moved from one latitude to the next. The Third World was trying to throw off its shackles, and the movement was gathering international momentum.

Algeria, too, was an example. On October 6, 1960, a manifesto signed by 121 French intellectuals was published in Paris, demanding the right to insubordination in Algeria. It was followed that same year, on December 19, by UN recognition of the Algerian people's right to independence. In March 1962, the French government signed the Evian accords with leaders of the Algerian insurrection, and Algeria gained its independence on July 3 of that year.

But the eyes of the world were once again focussed on the United States. Attention was drawn to the tensions produced by the proximity of a Communist regime in Cuba and by American involvement in Vietnam. Indignation against the social injustice affecting blacks and native

Americans and the refusal to accept it provided ideal subject matter for concerned and committed illustrators.

In Cuba, Che Guevara was the standard-bearer of revolutionary hopes. In Vietnam, it was Ho Chi Minh who played the same role, while in the United States, it was Martin Luther King. These emblematic figures often appeared in editorial illustrations.

In June 1963, the Governor of Arkansas allowed a few black students to enter the till then segregated university in Little Rock. The white population was so hostile that the students had to have a police escort. Television crews filmed the event, and suddenly small screens in living rooms across America were filled with white hate and fury against this "infamous" act. Reaction set in. That August, pastor Martin Luther King organized a civil rights march on Washington that drew two hundred thousand people.

During the early Sixties, the National Liberation Front was founded in Vietnam (December 1960). Though public opinion was not yet fully aware of it, it was the same type of struggle. By March 1962, the South Vietnamese were mounting operations against the Vietcong with the assistance of American military "advisors". Meanwhile, in the United States, the pace of events was picking up. When Martin Luther King was awarded the Nobel Peace Prize in 1964, it seemed to Europeans that things were taking a turn for the better, but racism was still too deeply rooted among a segment of the American population for it to be wiped out overnight.

In February 1965, the leader of the Black Muslims, Malcolm X, was assassinated. There followed a wave of racist terrorist acts against militants of the civil rights movement.

By August of that year, tension reached its peak as race riots broke out in Watts, the black community in Los Angeles. It heralded the rise of the Black Panther movement; in June

Paul Davis
"Martin Luther King". Cover of Rolling Stone, 1986.

1966, Stokely Carmichael launched the "Black Power" battle cry. Toni Ungerer caught the struggle in one of his drawings, showing the two "powers" devouring one another (see page 20). The summer of 1966 was "hot", marked in July by a rampage in Chicago during which Martin Luther King was wounded and by more rioting in San Francisco the following month.

A year later, in July 1977, fresh outbursts of violence took on major proportions in Newark and Detroit. The black movement was becoming more radical, and there was stronger determination not to back down. A few days before these riots, boxing champion Cassius Clay refused to be sworn in as he was about to be inducted into the American Army. (Clay had converted to Islam and joined the Black Muslims in 1964, taking the name of Muhammad Ali.) He was sentenced to five years in prison, thereby becoming a symbolic figure for black activists. But reactionaries had not given up the fight. On April 4, 1968, America learned with horror of the assassination in Memphis of Martin Luther King. A rising tide of fury engulfed the country, leaving forty-six dead and thousands wounded. American was stunned, and the rest of the world aghast. Muhammad Ali had set the example for other blacks by publicly rejecting American values. His act of defiance was imitated by two black runners during the Olympic Games of October 1968. Tommie Smith and John Carlos stepped up to the podium in Mexico City to receive their medals wearing black berets, black gloves and sunglasses. At the sound of the American national anthem, they lowered their heads and raised their fists, an act of provocation that staked their claim to dignity and autonomy but shocked the world. This was also the year of the famed month of May, a month that shook the Western world to its foundations. Students in Paris and Mexico, San Francisco and Warsaw, Milan and Prague went on the rampage, making for the most widespread movement in favour of autonomy, identity and the right to be different. These events were brilliantly rendered by such illustrators as Paul Davis and Tomi Ungerer.

An equally strong protest movement was gaining momentum against the Vietnam War. In August 1964, tension rose in the Gulf of Tongking between the American forces and the North Vietnamese. As time went on, the conflict that had been centred in South Vietnam saw North and South oppose one another, with the United States supporting the South and China the North.

A large proportion of American youth opposed what they considered to be a dirty war and condemned their leaders for taking such action. They were not the only ones. In April 1967, Martin Luther King widened the scope of his movement's concerns by organizing a peace march in front of the United Nations headquarters in New York. It drew over one hundred thousand demonstrators.

Paul Davis
"Supreme Court".
Look Magazine, 1966.

Paul Davis
Cover and
inside illustra-
tion for New
York Magazine,
November
1970.
"Black Against
Black : The
Agony of
Panthermania".

Paul Davis
Evergreen,
1969.
"The Fall of
Muhammad
Ali".

Paul Davis
Cover of
Sports
Illustrated,
May 1965.
"Cassius Clay
vs Sonny
Liston".

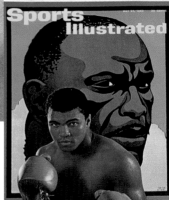

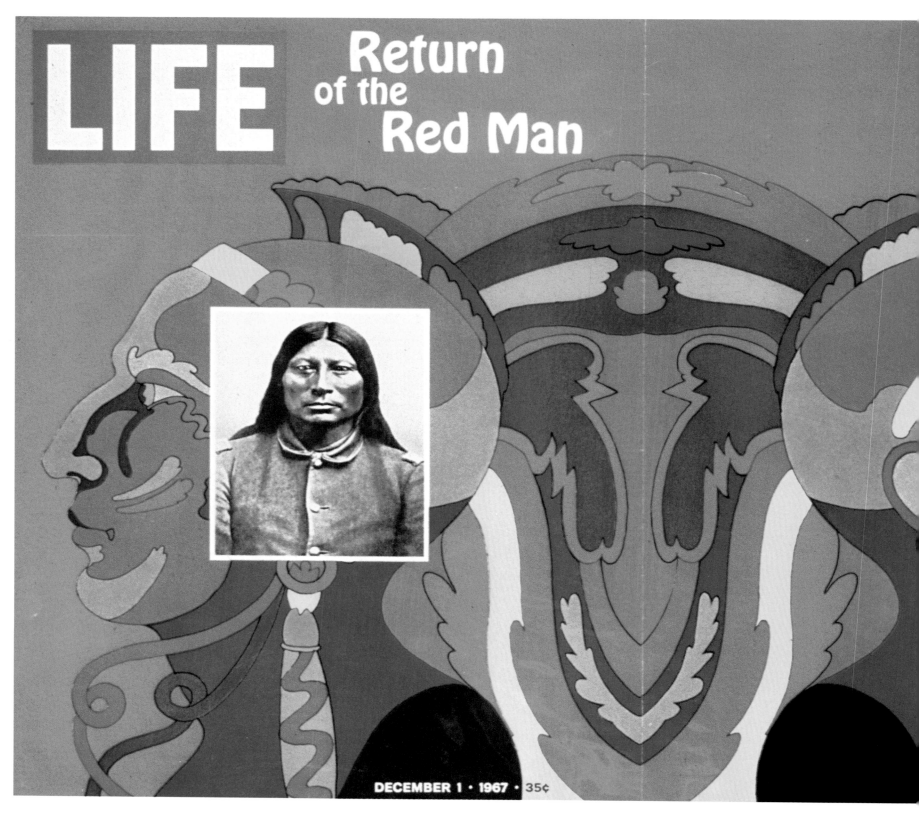

LIFE
Return of the Red Man

DECEMBER 1 · 1967 · 35¢

In November 1969, a crowd two-hundred-and-fifty thousand strong massed in front of the White House following the revelation of the brutal massacre of Vietnamese civilians in the village of My-Lai. More than twice that number marched on Washington to the cry of "Peace Now" in April 1971. Among them were many Vietnam veterans, some maimed, who threw their war medals onto a bonfire.

A young black professor of philosophy, Angela Davis, was put on trial for her pro-civil rights and anti-war activities. She was sentenced in 1970, and remained in prison till June 1972. During her time in jail, she became as famous a figure as Che Guevara.

Conflict was not confined to the United States. In September 1964, Palestinians in exile in Egypt announced the creation of a Palestinian army, and Yasser Arafat was named head of the Palestinian Liberation Organization.

Meanwhile, Che Guevara had quit Castro's side in disappointment and had joined revolutionary forces in Bolivia. On October 9, 1967, he was found dead under "mysterious" circumstances. In August 1969, a wave of terror swept over Ulster, killing nine people and wounding five hundred and fourteen. In June 1970, riots broke out in Belfast and Londonderry, setting off escalating violence in August 1971. Two years later, forty thousand people sacked the British Embassy in Dublin; in February 1976, the IRA militant Frank Stagg died in prison of self-imposed fasting. His death led to other outbursts, which Jean-Claude Castelli captured in a single illustration (page 30), a magnificent summing up of the Irish situation. In Vietnam, meanwhile, Saigon capitulated, and North and South Vietnam were reunited in June 1976.

In October 1970, Salvador Allende took power in Chile, setting up a revolutionary government. That same year, Jerry Rubin published "Do It", a book that attempted to draw a parallel between the hippie movement and the left-wing sentiments of revolutionary white youths. An immediate success, the book, with its preface by Black Panther leader Eldridge Cleaver, became a manifesto of the "Yippie" movement.

On the heels of black America came the "Red" awakening. The native American movement was extolled by Milton Glaser in his illustration called "Return of the Red Man" (at left) and by Paul Davis in "Indian Dream". In an unexpected twist, Marlon Brando refused to attend the Oscar awards ceremony in March 1973, sending a young Apache women to refuse the award in his place. In a strong voice, she read a declaration in which the actor affirmed his support for the rights of the Indian Nations. The Sioux Leonard Peltier and a handful of braves simultaneously undertook a siege of Wounded Knee in South Dakota. After 71 days, the leader of the "Red Power" movement, Russell Means, signed an agreement with the federal government. But that did not put an end to exactions and abuses. Rushed by the American Indian Movement to Pine Ridge, Leonard Peltier answered FBI provocations with firearms. Arrested in Canada, Peltier has remained in prison to this day.

Agitation rippled round the world. In Madrid, Basque separatists took the life of Franco's right-hand man, Admiral Luis Carrero-Blanco, on December 20, 1973. On January 30 of the following year, France outlawed Basque, Breton and Corsican autonomist organizations. April of the same year saw a bloodless revolution in Portugal.

In June 1976, riots in Soweto caused twenty-three deaths and wounded over two hundred people. In September 1978, the Sandinistas sparked a general insurrection in Nicaragua. The decade came to a close as it had begun, with recriminations, pressing demands and bloodshed. The election in October 1978 of a Pole as Pope John-Paul II lent impetus to liberation movements in Eastern European countries. On September 22, 1980, a Polish shipyard worker called Lech Walesa founded Solidarnosc, the first anti-establishment trade union in a Communist country.

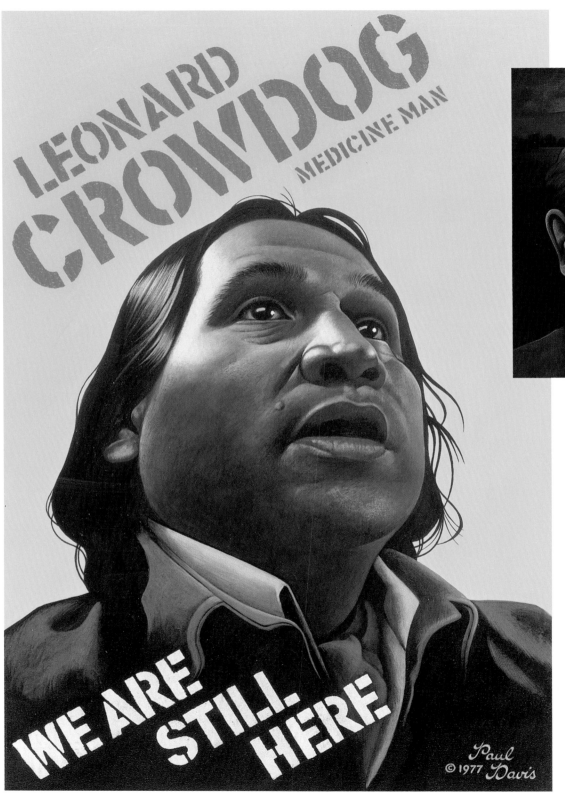

Paul Davis
"Indian Dream".
Poster in support of
George McGovern's
presidential campaign,
1972.

Paul Davis
"Leonard Crowdog".
Poster in support of
the American Indian
struggle, 1977.

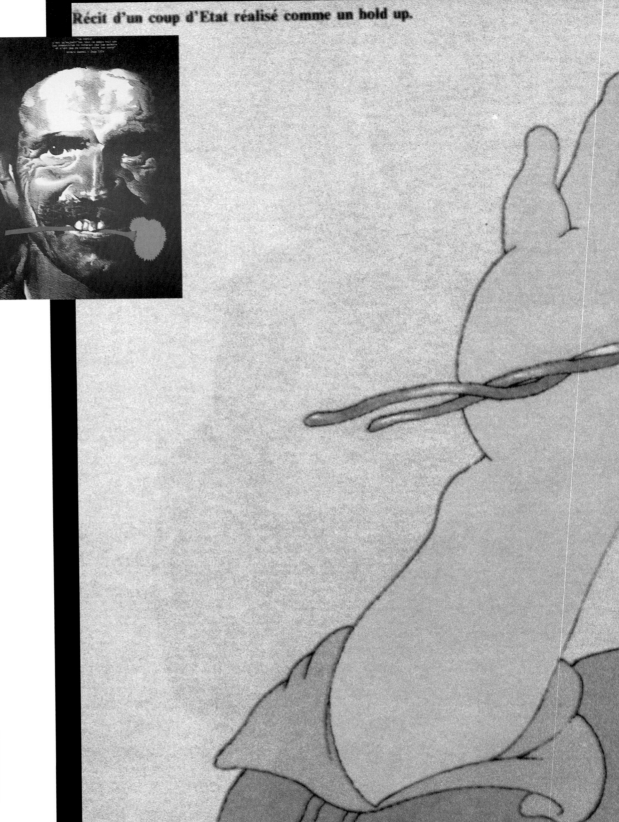

Philippe Corentin (far right) *Lui*, no. 131, December 1974. "Les chaînes qu'on abat", article devoted to the bloodless revolution in Portugal.

Michel Quarez (right) Poster in support of the bloodless revolution in Portugal (visual homage to "Los Borrachos" by Velasquez), 1976.

Jean-Claude Castelli (below) Cover design for a book on the IRA struggle in northern Ireland for Editions Champ Libre, 1969.

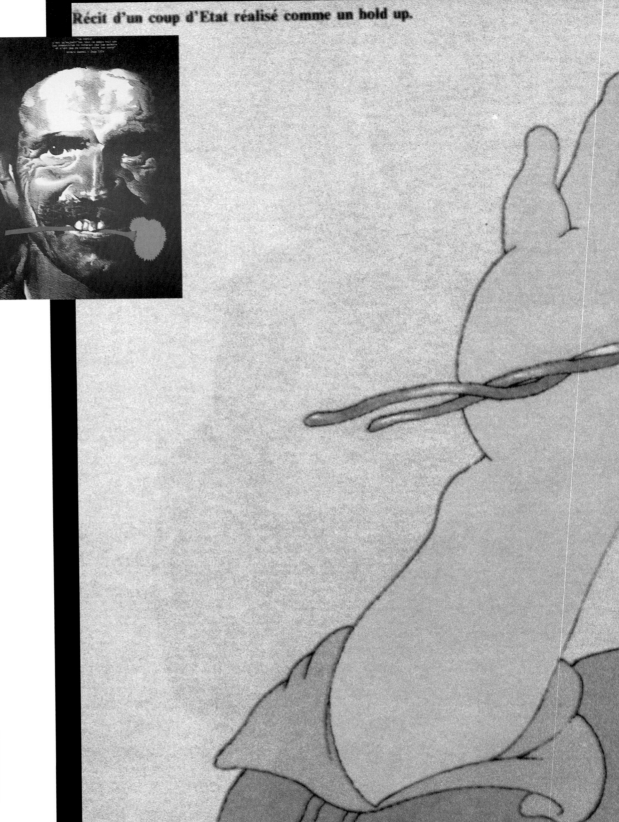

Récit d'un coup d'Etat réalisé comme un hold up.

LES CHAINES QU'O

Au Portugal, il a suffi d'une nuit pour que quarante-sept ans de dictature volen mando, tel un hold-up, a fait basculer le régime. En douceur. Voici. heure par he du 24 avril, par Pierre Audibert et Daniel Brignon, auteurs de « Portugal, les no

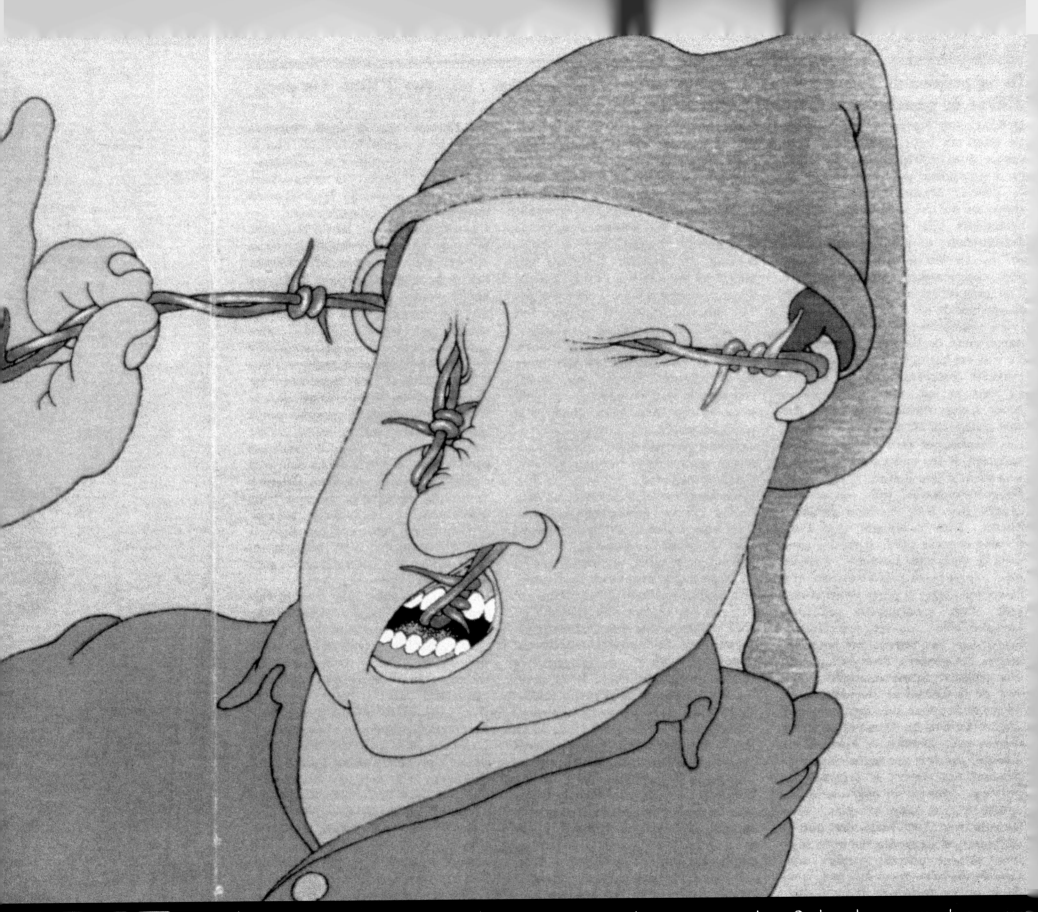

ABAT

ts. Une opération de com-
cit de cette nuit historique
centurions» chez Belfond

Lisbonne est, ce soir, peuplée d'om-
bres. Cette nuit du 24 au 25 avril
est une nuit comme tant d'autres,
pourtant. Des voitures parcourent les
artères de la capitale portugaise. Les
« couche-tard », boivent le dernier

verre. En ce printemps, un peu de
bonheur s'étend sur cette ville an-
cienne et belle. Sur les ondes des
radios, les disques se succèdent. On
fredonne les airs à la mode. On s'en-
dort parfois. L'existence est ordinaire

Quelques hommes attendent pourtant
l'extraordinaire. L'oreille collée au
récepteur de radio, ils écoutent la
station Radio-Renaissance. Ils res-
semblent aux résistants de l'ombre qui
durant la dernière guerre écoutaient

Michel Quarez
Esquire, 1972.
Illustration for an
article on the
Vietnam War,
accompanied by
a Shakespeare
quote : "What is
honour, a
word…"

Spiralling Violence

It was and is still not easy to draw the line between struggles for liberation and all the other sources of violence that proliferated during those schizophrenic years. Many terrorist acts were "justified" by putting the blame on the rigidity of people and institutions; they were perpetrated in the name of so-called "revolutionary virtues". Yet illustrators with such widely varying styles and political commitments as Quarez (page 32), Glaser, Ungerer (pages 33, 34), Lagarrigue (page 35), Topor (page 39), McMullan, Le Saux (page 39) and Corentin had to trace that nearly impalpable line each time they dealt with an event.

Hardly a day went by during the Sixties and Seventies without an international event pointing to the entrenchment of dictatorships in Spain, the Soviet Union and the satellite countries; the rise of totalitarian regimes in Chile, Uganda, Brazil, Central Africa, Argentina, Ethiopia, Greece and Libya; open warfare in Vietnam and the Middle East or undeclared war in Angola and Cambodia; the rise of urban violence as well as various forms of terrorism (assassinations, airplane hijackings, hostage-taking, and kidnappings, not to mention putschs).

The first barricades went up in the streets of Algiers in November 1960, heralding the putsch organized by a handful of French generals in April 1961 and the creation of the right-wing, colonialist Organization de l'Armée Secrète (OAS or Secret Army Organization). When Parisians took to the streets to demonstrate against the OAS on February 8, 1962, the intervention of a riot police squad resulted in eight deaths. These deaths may quite possibly have shocked the French Government into speeding up negotiations with the Algerian liberation movement, for the Evian Accords were signed barely one month later. Despite the granting of independence to Algeria, France's policy on North Africa did not radically change. A case in point was the kidnapping of Algerian leader Mehdi Ben Barka at a street corner in Saint-Germain-des-Près in Paris on October 30, 1965. Less than six months after President Kennedy proclaimed "Ich bin ein Berliner" in front of the Berlin Wall in June 1963, and a mere twenty-one days after he tacitly approved the putsch that killed the then Vietnamese President, Diem, he in turn was assassinated on a sunny November day in Dallas. That same year, Stanley Kubrick produced his film "Dr. Strangelove", which was a powerful condemnation of man's madness to willingly engage in nuclear war. Meanwhile, Francesco Rosi denounced financial corruption in his film "Le mani sulla cita". The indictment was clear, but how many people actually got the message?

An equally clear message, this time about Vietnam, was given by French film-maker Pierre Schoendoerffer in 1964, with his film "317ème Section". The fighting there was officially proclaimed a war on November 7. Within a few months, the fighting was stepped up. In April the first napalm bombs were dropped.

(That same month, US marines landed in Santo Domingo, as if to make the public forget the ill-conceived landing in Cuba's Bay of Pigs.)

In June 1966, General Thieu became President of South Vietnam. A year later, the northern cities of Hanoi and Haiphong were mercilessly bombarded. (Meanwhile, Mao Tse-tung launched the disastrous Cultural Revolution that let loose bands of young Red Guards who were known to beat their professors and destroy art works. In June 1967, the Chinese successfully launched their first A-bomb.) Shortly before the new presidential election was to be held, President Johnson decided to halt the bombings of North Vietnam and to enter into negotiations. It was too late, for Richard Nixon won the election. He finally withdrew thirty-five thousand American troops from the Vietnam battlefields in September 1969, but that did not prevent him from surreptitiously bombing

Tomi Ungerer
Militant poster against US military involvement in Vietnam. 1967.

Cambodia in May 1970. Nonetheless, the peace process gradually gained momentum.

On January 27, 1971, at the Hotel Majestic in Paris, Henry Kissinger and Le Duc-Tho sat down together to sign a cease-fire agreement. Two months later, the last GI quit Vietnamese soil, leaving behind a bloodied land of lamentation. The war the United States lost had cost it some one hundred and thirty-five billion dollars and fifty-six thousand lives.

On April 23, 1973, the Cambodian city of Phnom-Penh was encircled by the Red Khmer soldiers of the blood-thirsty dictator Pol Pot.

As the years rolled by, the list of bloodlettings got longer and longer. In 1965, generals took power in Indonesia, signalling the systematic slaughter of Communists there. In the Central African Republic, Jean Bedel Bokassa, who was not yet a self-styled emperor, grabbed power. In 1967, General Gowon took power in Nigeria; Colonels Papadopoulos and Patakos did the same in Greece. The Six Day War pitted Israel against Egypt, Syria and Jordan.

The year 1968 raised great hopes. The uprisings in what came to be known as the Prague Springtime were crushed by Soviet tanks sent under cover of the Warsaw Pact. In Mexico City, the police shot at student demonstrators, killing dozens. On June 6, Robert Kennedy was assassinated in Los Angeles by Sirhan Sirhan. In August and September, the world watched in horror as hundreds of thousands were exterminated in Biafra. In December, General Costa e Silva instigated a putsch in Brazil.

The year 1969 began with the self-immolation by fire of a young Prague student named Jan Pallach. In Libya, Colonel Kadhafi took over, while in India grave religious disorders resulted in six hundred deaths. But what was most striking that year was the intensification of plane hijackings, giving rise to a new sort of terrorism.

The following year, a Palestinian organization called the Popular Front for the Liberation of Palestine perpetrated five hijackings as well as an attack on an Israeli school bus, killing eight children and wounding twenty-one others. The increasingly brutal violence worried not only Palestinian enemies but their allies as well. In Jordan, King Hussein cracked down on unruly Palestinian organizations in bloody "Black September". In Spain, the sentences handed down at the Burgos trial, death by garroting, set off a wave of international indignation against Franco and his fascist regime. The rule of violence continued to pertain in 1971. The coup d'état of Idi Ami Dada in Uganda was a bloodbath, while an atrocious war in Bengal provoked a mass exodus and killed over half a million people, accompanied by a particularly fierce cholera epidemic.

Gratuitous violence was becoming ever more common-place, hitting individuals as well as communities. That was the thrust of Stanley Kubrick's memorable film "Clockwork Orange", based on the novel by Anthony Burgess. On February 26, 1972, a Maoist militant by the name of Pierre Overney was killed by a private guard at the Renault car factory outside Paris. The funeral services drew a huge crowd. In Italy on March 14, publisher Gianfranco Feltrinelli, who was closely connected with far-left factions, was found dead; the bizarre circumstances surrounding his death and the discovery of the corpse were never elucidated.

The climate in Italy became extremely tense as a string of unpredictable terrorist acts was committed by the Mafia, the Red Brigades and the fascist organization Black Order. In August 1974, the latter claimed credit for a series of attacks, the most serious of which was the bombing of a Rome-Munich train, that killed twelve and wounded forty-eight. In March 1978 Aldo Moro was kidnapped

Tomi Ungerer
"Kiss for peace".
Poster, 1967.

Seymour Chwast
"End bad breath".
Poster, 1965.

Jean Lagarrigue
Cover of New York
Magazine, 1975.
"The Hidden War in
Cambodia".

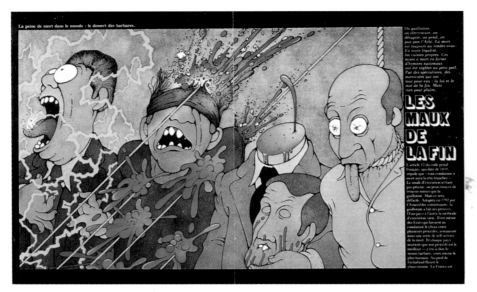

Philippe Corentin
Lui, no. 163, August 1977.
"Les maux de la fin",
article on the death penalty.

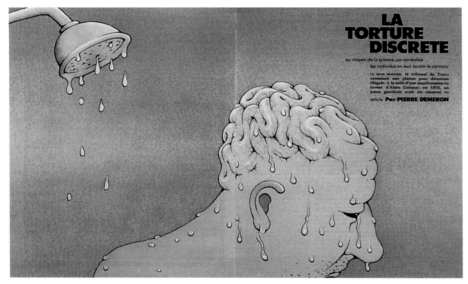

**Philippe
Corentin**
Playboy
France,
no. 42,
May 1977.

the German manufacturing association, Hans Martin Schleyer, was found dead in the trunk of an Audi near the Franco-German border. One of the most horrifying terrorist attacks occurrred during the Olympic Games held in Munich in September 1972: eleven young athletes in the Israeli team were murdered by a Palestinian commando group.

It was indeed a time of spiralling violence, without rhyme or reason. Around the world came a quick succession of brutal incidents by governments and individuals: putsches and uprisings, terrorist acts and repression. Though each new outbreak of violence seemed totally unconnected with previous one, there was an underlying similitude.

Belfast and Londonderry flared up in July 1972. In September 1973, Pinochet took power in Chile, and the world nearly witnessed Allende being shot to death. The Yom Kippur War in October 1973 once again pitted Israel against Syria and Egypt; the Catalan anarchist Puig-Antich was garrotted in March 1974; a terrorist bombing of Le Drugstore in Saint-Germain-des-Près in July left two dead and thirty-four wounded; in November, a bomb planted in Birmingham by the IRA killed nineteen persons and wounded two hundred. In 1975, civil war broke out in Lebanon, while in Corsica, autonomists held a violent demonstration in Bastia. In early 1976 thirty children were kidnapped in Djibouti by the Somali Coast Liberation Front. Meanwhile, fifteen thousand Cuban "advisors" landed in Angola. In July, would-be hijackers were temporarily discouraged after Israeli shock troops executed a brilliant rescue operation of the hostages held at Entebbe. Red terror struck at the heart of Addis-Abeba in Ethiopa in February 1977. In November 1978, the tragedy of the Vietnamese boat people reached its apogee when the Indonesian government refused to let the two thousand five hundred and seventeen passengers on board the Hai-Hong disembark. The year 1979 was like a fireworks display of violence: in January, Vietnamese troops invaded Cambodia; in February, war broke out between China and Vietnam; in November, a terrorist bomb in Mecca caused the death of two hundred and forty-four pilgrims; and in December, Soviet troops invaded Afghanistan.

The Seventies proved then to be a decade of bloodshed and ruin. The Eighties were about as bloody, with the outbreak of war between Iran and Irak in September 1980.

by the Red Brigades. His corpse was discovered in the trunk of a car on May 9. The principal leader of the brigade, Renato Curcio, was sentenced to fifteen years in prison on June 23.

In Germany, the Baader gang was making headlines. Four gang members, Andreas Baader, Holger Meins, Jan-Karl Raspe and Gudurn Ensslin, were arrested in 1972 and were put on trial in May 1975. The proceedings dragged on until March 1977, when the four were sentenced to life imprisonment. That October, the gang committed "suicide" in a Stuttgart prison or, as the saying went at the time, "were suicided": Baader and Raspe died of bullet wounds, Ensslin of hanging. A young woman by the name of Irmgard Möller, who had been sentenced later, was found seriously wounded. It seemed as if institutional violence had won out over individual violence, but the following day the head of

Jean Lagarrigue
Playboy France,
October 1975.
"Les corruptibles
de Chicago",
on corruption.

Roland Topor
Cover
of Szpilki
(Warsaw), on
censorship,
1974.

Michel Quarez
Poster in support
of a workers'
sit-in strike
at the
Parisien Libéré.
1975.

Pierre Le-Tan
Postcard in support
of Solidarnocz trade union
outlawed by the Polish
government, 1980.

Alain Le Saux
Poster on unemployment
for the French Socialist
Party's election campaign
for the European
Parliament, 1979.

Philippe Corentin
Lui, no. 216, January
1982. "Magnum:
et que ça saute!",
article on the police.

Philippe Corentin
Lui, no. 227,
December 1982.
"Le péril jeune",
article devoted to
rising juvenile
deliquence
in Italy.

Alain Le Saux
Lui, no. 195,
April 1980.
"La voix
de la liberté",
article on the
intervention of
psychologists
during
hostage-
taking.

**James
McMullan**
Esquire,
July 1978.
Article on the Baader-
Meinhoff gang.

Alain Le Saux
Lui, no. 184,
May 1979.
"Mort aux
lâches", article
devoted to
anti-terrorist
brigades in
Great Britain.

41

Philippe Corentin

Lui, no. 205, February 1981
"L'ai-je bien descendu?",
article denouncing violence
in sports stadiums. Sports,
and particularly soccer games,
became so important politically
and economically that a team
had to win at any cost.

On ne joue plus la balle, on joue le bonhomme. Le sport d'équipe, aujourd'hui, ça fait mal. La castagne, au rugby, ce n'est pas nouveau; ce qui l'est, c'est le record de pattes cassées au foot. Pauvres sportifs : si on nous les brise...

Un méchant coup de coude lors d'un plaquage. Un joueur qui se venge salement en visant le bas-ventre d'un adversaire. Sous la douleur, monstrueuse, Serge Gabernet, arrière international, est plié en deux. La douleur s'estompe peu après, pour revenir

PAR RENAUD DE LABORDERIE BILAN TRAGIQUE DE LA VIOLENCE SUR LES STADES

L'AI-JE BIEN DESCENDU?

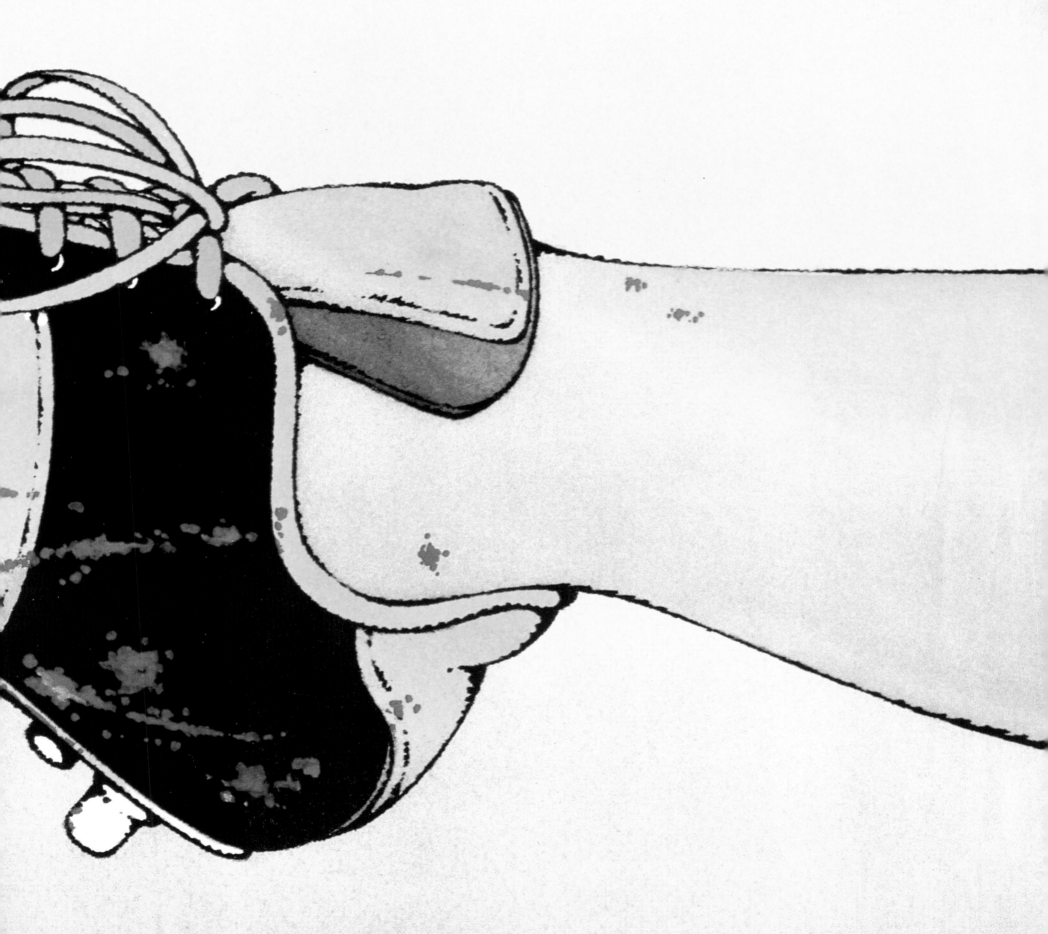

Paul Davis
Cover of
Evergreen, 1968.

The Faces of Power

A sea-change occurred during the Sixties. Respect for institutions was dying; as for reverence, it had become an antiquated notion.

Till then caricaturists had had a quasi-monopoly on visual pamphleteering. To all extent and purposes, a head of state or leaders of any kind or degree of power were not to be bandied about. The only major exception, the only acceptable vehicle for letting off steam was caricatures, usually confined to political publications.

Glossy magazines were eminently respectable, prized for their beautiful four-colour reproductions and high quality, large-format paper; generally speaking, they were as well bred as young ladies at a tea party. And then, almost overnight, they converted to disrespect.

Readers discovered full pages or double-page spreads in colour that showed the hitherto carefully hidden face of power: oppression, manipulation, malfeasance, corruption—nothing was considered off bounds. The tone was bantering, but all the more efficacious for that very reason. This was not preaching to believers but converting those who were still blind to the truth by showing up the malfunctioning of society.

No one was spared: crowned heads, military leaders, ecclesiastics, hatted heads and even shaved heads. The one exception, and a major one at that, was Ernesto Guevara, an Argentinian doctor who became a Cuban political leader during the three-year revolution (from 1956 to 1959) that brought Fidel Castro and his "barbudos" to power. Guevara tired rather quickly of the ins and outs of political power and the inroads made into dogma for pragmatic purposes. He left Cuba to pursue his revolutionary ideals elsewhere, and was assassinated in Bolivia on October 9, 1967.

The "guerrillero heroico" became a figure of legend, an absolutely untouchable icon. Latin Americans from Angel Parra to Carlos Puebla, and from Atahualpa Yupanqui to Soledad Bravo all sang his praises with cries of "Hasta siempre" and "El Che vive". The "icon" was captured forever by Paul Davis on the cover of Evergreen magazine (see opposite page) and then by Roman Cieslewicz on the cover of Opus (see this page).

Leaders around the world were getting their due, up to and including President Mao, who had usually been kept out of the general free-for-all. Cieslewicz struck once again, as only he could do, with a highly ambiguous "Mona Tse Tung", whereas Jean-Paul Goude poked fun in Esquire at one of the grand gestures of the Chinese Cultural Revolution (1966-1976): the figure of China's great leader Mao swimming across the Yellow River alongside a loopy-looking Donald Duck made of bright yellow plastic (see page 47).

Alain Le Saux used his biting sense of humour to tackle the wooden, stereotyped language preferred by political leaders in the Popular Republics of Eastern Europe. It was a stylistic exercise that corresponded nicely with the fresh reading of Marx that had begun a few years earlier (pages 48-49).

People were discovering bigger and bigger cracks in the foundations of Marxism, and even the famous trio of Marx, Lenin and Stalin was coming in for a barrage of criticism. Despite the fact that Michel Quarez had a reputation for orthodox thinking, he nonetheless depicted the founding-father figure of Marx as a hitch-hiker. Pascalini portrayed Lenin with an outrageous layer of make-up on his face. And during the trials of the Prague insurrectionists, Jean-Claude Castelli showed up Stalin, the Father of the People, for what he was (page 50).

Dictators and putschists, of which there was no dearth, were perfect targets for the great illustrators. Before he died on January 22, 1971, François Duvalier, the infamous Haitian dic-

Roman Cieslewicz
Cover of Opus no. 3, 1968.

tator nicknamed "Papa Doc", came under the sharp eye of Castelli. Kadhafi took power on September 1, 1969, and Juan Peron made a temporary comeback as dictator of Argentina during the autumn of 1973. Bokassa came to power in the Central African Republic in 1971 and got himself crowned emperor, under the benevolent gaze of the French government, on December 4, 1977. Idi Amin Dada took power in Uganda in January 1971. He fled to Libya at the end of his eight-year reign, leaving behind a bloody record: three hundred thousand dead. In the wake of decolonization, Africa was plagued by ethnic and tribal conflicts that often stemmed directly from the disputed borders of the former colonial territories, which provided perfect opportunities for aspiring dictators.

Endemic evil was not confined to the African continent. In December 1970, Franco drew the eyes of the world to Spain during the trials held in Burgos. In Latin America, Pinochet came to power in Chile in September 1973, and Videla in Argentina in the spring of 1976. Trouble was also brewing in the West. Though President Nixon's meeting with Mao Tse Tung in Peking on February 21, 1972, raised great expectations, the publication by the Washington Post of the Watergate scandal was hard to stomach, and illustrators like Paul Davis (page 54), Roland Topor and Seymour Chwast let loose their indignation. Among the many vicissitudes of the Seventies, one dictatorship came to an end with the death of Franco in November 1975, but the bloodthirsty leader of the Red Khmers, Pol Pot, was named head of "democratic" Kampuchea in April 1976. Egyptian President Anouar el Sadate became the first Arab head of state to be invited to and actually go to Israel: in November 1977, he addressed the Knesset. But in July 1979, Saddam Hussein took over in Irak. Though Mao Tse Tung disappeared from the Chinese scene in July 1976, the Ayatollah Khomeiny returned in triumph to Iran in February 1979.

On December 13, 1980, General Jaruzelski, President of the Polish Military Council, outlawed the Solidarnosc trade union. In Rome, another Pole, Karol Wojtyla, was elected Pope John Paul II in 1978. He was soon confronted by the scandal of the Ambrosiano Bank, and Philippe Corentin took obvious pleasure in pinpointing the dubious financial practises of the

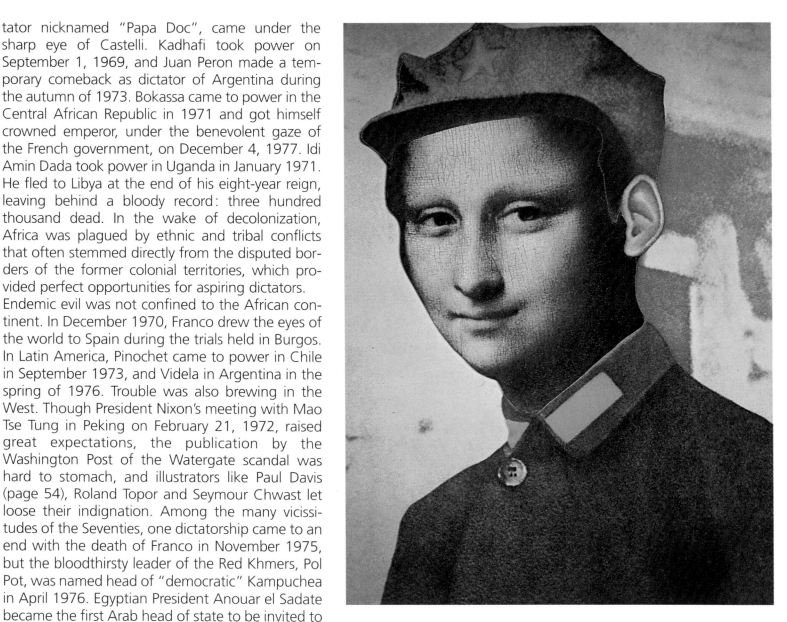

Roman Cieslewicz
"Mona Tse Tung".
Collage, 1977.

Vatican (pages 56-57). The political leaders who managed to escape the scathing commentary of magazine illustrators were few and far between. Even Queen Elizabeth was poked fun at by Jean Lagarrigue, while Margaret Thatcher drew the sarcasm of Gabriel Pascalini with "My Fer Lady" ("fer" means "iron" in English, as can be seen on page 55).

Thanks to these illustrators, the faults and foibles of those in the public eye became public knowledge. Their revelations were always handled with humour, which explains why readers found them so bright, clear and striking as to become unforgettable.

Jean-Paul Goude
Esquire, 1970. "Mao ou en remontant le Fleuve Jaune", or Mao's exploit swimming across the Yellow River.

Following page

Alain Le Saux
Lui, no. 159, April 1977. "Déraison d'état", article on the stereotyped, "wooden" language of Communist regimes.

47

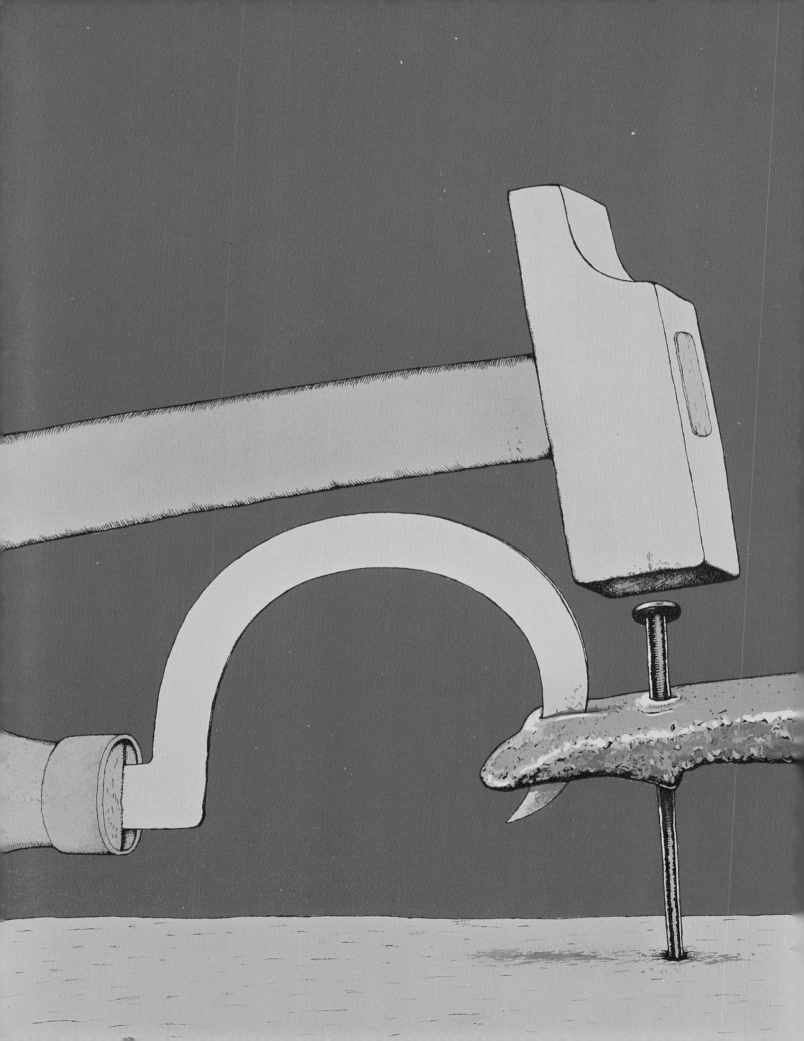

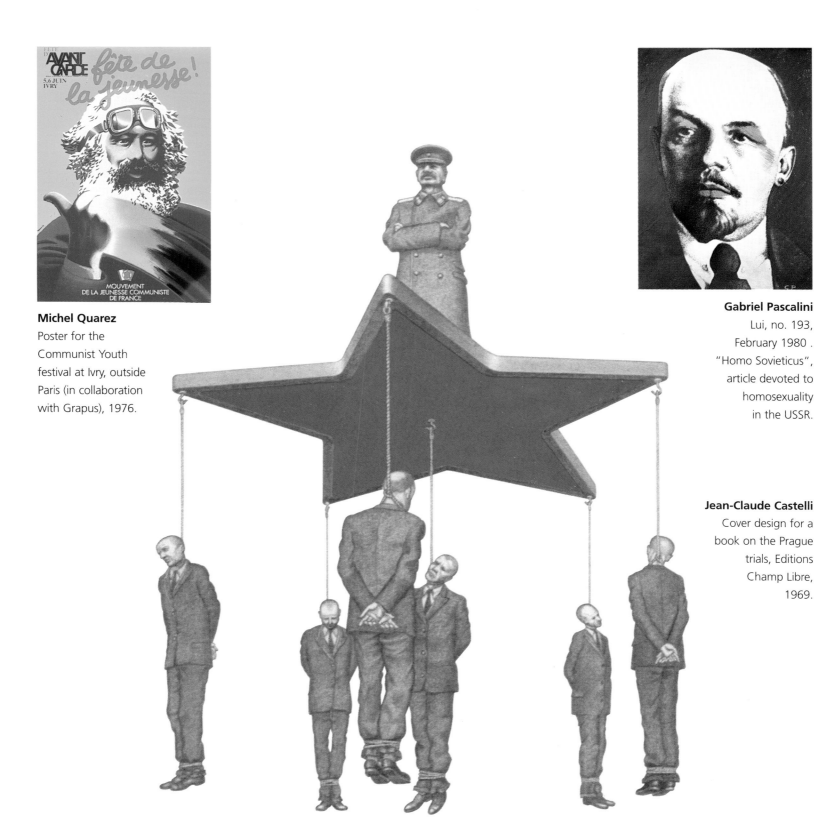

Michel Quarez
Poster for the Communist Youth festival at Ivry, outside Paris (in collaboration with Grapus), 1976.

Gabriel Pascalini
Lui, no. 193, February 1980 . "Homo Sovieticus", article devoted to homosexuality in the USSR.

Jean-Claude Castelli
Cover design for a book on the Prague trials, Editions Champ Libre, 1969.

Jean-Claude Castelli
Lui, no. 74, March 1970.
"François Duvalier,
un Haïtien haï des siens",
or the hated Haitian dictator.

Jean Lagarrigue
Lui, no. 127, August
1974. "Fürher noir",
article devoted to
Idi Amin Dada.

Philippe Corentin
Lui, no. 153, October
1976. "Putsch, je passe",
article on the dictatorship
of General Pinochet
in Chile.

Tract
Poster, 1975.

LIBERTÉ CHILI

Jean-Claude Castelli
Lui, no. 94,
November 1971.
"Amour, castagnettes
et Franco"

52

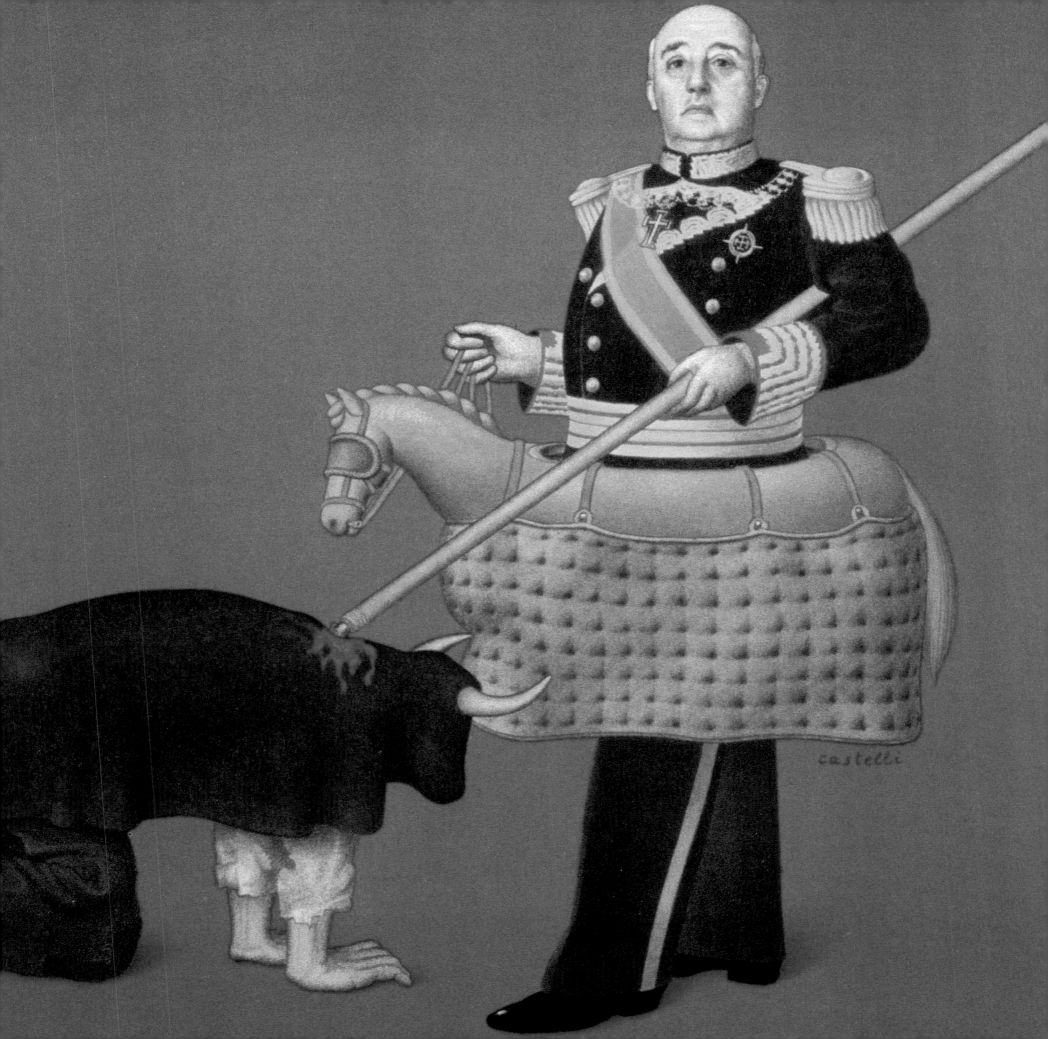

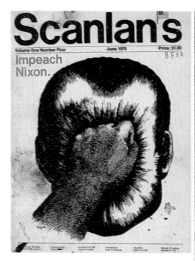

Roland Topor
Cover of Scanlans
(United States),
June 1970.
A vengeful fist in
Nixon's face.

Paul Davis
Cover of New York
Magazine, 1971.
About keeping an
eye on Nixon two
years before the
Watergate scandal.
In spite of his
diplomatic
successes,
American liberals
doubted the
President's honesty
and loyalty.

Gabriel Pascalini
Lui, no. 222,
July 1982.
"My Fer Lady"
("fer" means "iron"),
portrait of
Margaret Thatcher,
Britain's iron-fisted
Prime Minister.

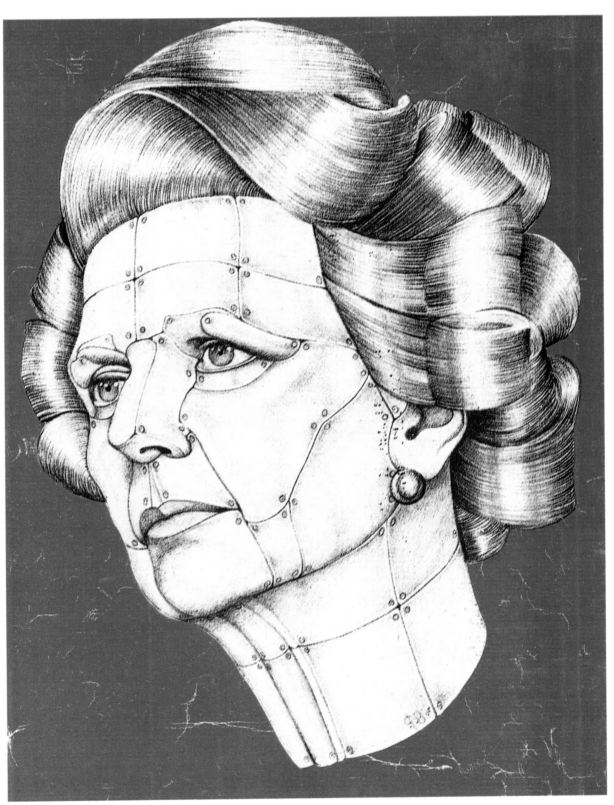

Jean Lagarrigue
Lui, no. 106,
November 1972.
"Sacré France
Dimanche", article
on the scandal-
mongering press.

Philippe Corentin
Lui, no. 226,
November 1982.
"Saint Père à l'oseille".
An article on the financial
scandals that shook the
Vatican in the early Eighties.

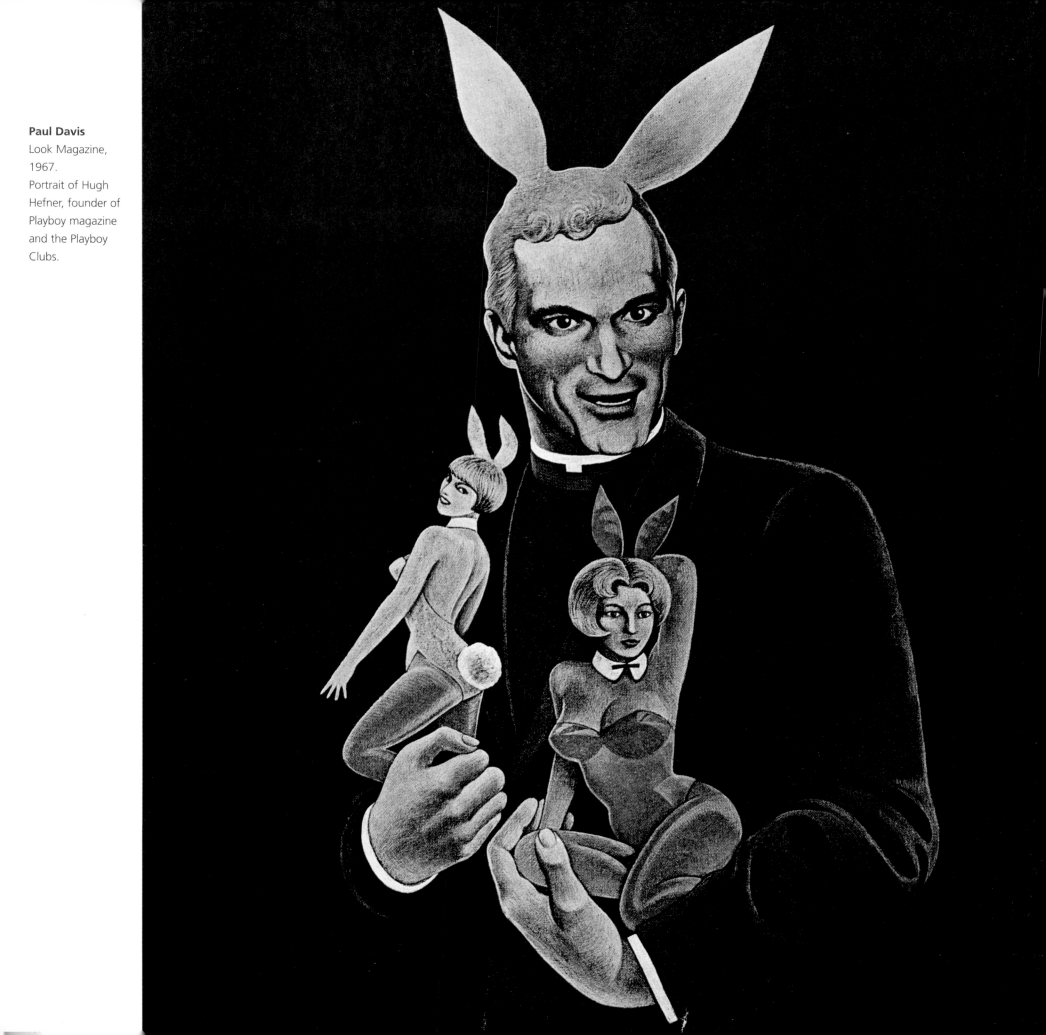

Paul Davis
Look Magazine, 1967.
Portrait of Hugh Hefner, founder of Playboy magazine and the Playboy Clubs.

Women On the March

The publication in 1963 of Betty Friedan's "The Feminine Mystique" was like a clap of thunder signalling the start of the Feminist storm, which was to gain momentum throughout the Sixties and Seventies. Translated into numerous languages, her book sold two million copies. While Hugh Heffner was brilliantly promoting the image of women as sex objects in his magazine Playboy and affiliated nightclubs, Betty Friedan laid bare the sources of the deepseated dissatisfaction of the typical postwar housewife.

The decade had begun with the début of Tina Turner and the exploits of the "black gazelle" Wilma Rudolph, who walked off with three gold medals at the Olympic Games in Mexico. That same year, the first contraceptive pill was put on the market in the United States. In 1962, fans around the world were deeply saddened by the death of Marilyn Monroe, who was not merely a glamorous sex symbol for millions of men but also an emblem of human frailty for men and women alike. That same year, women invaded the fashion world as the French were given a taste of truly stylish ready-to-wear with up-and-coming designers like Christiane Bailly, Emmanuelle Khanh, Michèle Rosier, the Jacobsons under the Dorothée Bis label, Maïmé Arnodin and Denise Fayolle.

But it was in 1963 that women really became aware that theirs was a specific struggle for liberation, similar to other liberation movements around the world, and that there was a budding international network based on solidarity among women. On August 28, a huge crowd of feminists, organized by intellectuals, gathered together in front of the White House in Washington, where a gifted young singer by the name of Joan Baez stepped up to the microphone. This was one of the many causes that Baez was to commit to. Her songs became anthems of the civil rights movements,

and she actively participated in the protest against the Vietnam War, going so far as to travel to North Vietnam, which was being bombed by the American Army, on Christmas 1972.

It was at that time that women in Iran and Kenya were given the right to vote. While Betty Friedan and Joan Baez were in the forefront of the feminist movement in the United States, the story was very different in the Soviet Union. True, Valentina Terechkowa was the first woman to be sent into outer space. But her exploit did not herald feminist inroads into a stultified system. She was rather a token image, for Russian society under the Communist regime remained extremely conservative, paying lip service only to women's liberation. While men in the West were learning how to become helpmates, men in the Soviet Union continued to let their wives do all the housework, shopping and childcare on top of their regular jobs. Elsewhere, outstanding women were making their mark but they often served as alibis for not budging. The Sixties and Seventies saw the nomination of several women prime ministers : Indira Ghandi in India (in 1966), Golda Meir in Israel (in 1969), and Margaret Thatcher in Great Britain (in 1979). The young Bernadette Devlin was elected from Londonderry to the British Parliament. In France, two young women broke barriers at two of the most prestigious schools in the country : Françoise Chandernagor graduated first in her class at the Ecole Nationale d'Administration, which trains top civil servants, and Anne Chopin entered the all-male Ecole Polytechnique. Also in France, author Marguerite Yourcenar was the first woman to be elected to the Académie Française (in 1980).

In point of fact, women's stuggle for liberation did not have very much to do with individual success stories, which men are so apt to prize. The feminist movement had much more

"Right on sisters" Militant sticker widely distributed on the West Coast of the USA during the late Sixties and early Seventies.

to do with imposing new ideas and attitudes and with pushing through new legislation. Marching behind Betty Friedan came phalanxes of women writers to carry on the battle. Kate Millet's "Sexual Politics" laid theoretical foundations for the feminist movement, followed a few weeks later by the publication of Germaine Greer's "The Female Eunuch". In 1973 came Erica Jong's scandalous but hilarious "Fear of Flying", that forcefully staked out claims for women's intellectual and sexual integrity. The South African writer Doris Lessing, who had emigrated to London, produced the psychologically revealing "The Golden Notebook" in 1976. In France, Antoinette Fouque, who was the leader of a radical splinter group in the Women's Lib movement called "Psychanalyse et Politique", set up the first all-female publishing house. Les éditions Des Femmes got off to a flying start with the publication of "Du Côté des Petites Filles" by Elena Gianini Belotti.

What women wear or want to wear can be extremely revealing. The date of the first miniskirt is July 10, 1974. Mary Quandt in Great Britain and André Courrèges in France were the standard bearers of the new "liberated" look in fashion. The only magazine closely tied to the feminist movement that proved a commercial success was Ms., whose editor-in-chief was the beautiful, very photogenic Gloria Steinem. She popularized advanced feminist ideas, taking the opposite course from a magazine like Mademoiselle Age Tendre, launched in Paris in 1964. Ms. became an outstanding vehicle for the best illustrators, including Hedda Johnson, Barbara Nessim and Miriam Wosk (see pages 66 to 69).

On the legislative front, the advancement of feminist causes was coming on apace, even though it did not keep up with feminist demands. In 1964 the US Congress passed a law forbidding sexual discrimination. (For some Europeans, that law seemed to have been singularly perverted by cases of sexual harassment during the Nineties.) In 1965, the French Parliament granted women professional independence and the discretionary right to make use of their own monies and property. The Vatican II Council decreed that discrimination was contrary to God's will. In late 1967, it took a law passed in Parliament to finally give French women access to modern contraceptive devices and the pill. Simultaneously, English women obtained the right to have an abortion. The position of the Catholic Church, however, was ultra-conservative as far as contraceptive devices were concerned, and especially the pill. Even so, the Italian Parliament managed to pass a law that abolished punishment for adultery. In 1972 the

United States voted the most liberal abortion law at that time. The French Parliament had to go through a very tough political battle before finally adopting a law on December 4, 1974, that authorized abortion. A logical consequence was that the sale of contraceptives to minors became legal.

The United Nations got around to acknowledging this struggle by designating 1975 as Women's Year. In 1979, the first international conference on excision was held in Khartoum, in the Sudan, but that same year the Islamic regime in Iran forced women by law to wear a chador.

Elsewhere, the struggle for women's rights was becoming organized. In the USA, the National Organization for Women (NOW) came into being in 1966 and gradually grew to some six hundred thousand members strong. Big demonstrations against rape were organized in 1968. The struggle took on many forms. On June 3, Valerie Solanas, who had

Jean Lagarrigue
Lui, n°161,
January 1977.
"Le mâle
à la gorge",
article on Linda
Lovelace, heroine
of the film
"Deep Throat".

Patrick Arlet
Lui, no. 106,
November
1972.
"By appoint-
ment only"
love by tele-
phone.

Philippe Corentin
Lui, no. 206, March 1981. "A la queue Lulu" an article on women's sexual fantasies.

written the SCUM Manifesto (Society for Cutting Up Men), shot and seriously wounded Andy Warhol as a theatrical gesture to call attention to the cause. September 7, 1968, saw the official launching of Women's Lib, whose members brandished Simone de Beauvoir's "The Second Sex" like a bible and drew their analyses from the New Left's reinterpretation of Marxism and psychoanalysis. That same day, in the same city of Atlanta, Georgia, a component group of Women's Lib called WITCH (Women's International Terrorist Conspiracy) held a noisy demonstration against the election of Miss America. With this splashy send-off, the women's movement got seriously underway, with groups forming both in America and abroad.

August 26, 1970, was a day for demonstrations on either side of the Atlantic. In New York, fifty thousand women marched down Fifth Avenue demanding equality, while in Paris women laid a wreath on the tomb of the Unknown Soldier with a streamer stating: "There is someone even less known than the Unknown Soldier: his wife!" That year, French women founded their own equivalent of Women's Lib (Mouvement pour la Libération de la Femme or MLF), whose slogan was "One man out of two is a woman!"

These diverse groups dealt with all types of concerns for all types of women, whatever their origin or age. In 1971, Maggie Kuhn founded the Grey Panthers in New York, an idea that was quickly put into practise in Europe, and especially in Germany. Senior citizens were active participants in the feminist movement; by a neat coincidence Hal Ashby's film "Harold and Maude", the delightful love story of an eighty-year-old woman and a twenty-year-old boy, hit the screen. Women were gradually getting closer, at least in writing, to their goals of equal rights and sexual freedom. In France it was the fight for freedom of choice that fired the strongest commitments and drew the most fire in 1971. A left-wing newsweekly, Le Nouvel Observateur, published a manifesto signed by 343 women, some famous, some not, who admitted to having had an abortion. This became the founding stone of the Mouvement pour la Liberté de l'Avortement or MLA, which spearheaded the drive to abolish an old law that sent to jail those who practised, abetted or underwent an abortion. The highly publicized Bobigny trial of a seventeen-year-old girl who had had an abortion and who got off free thanks to feminist arguments made women everywhere aware of their growing power and of the need to control their own bodies and minds.

Women were present on other fronts. The spread of pornography was exasperating: in Germany, the Red Witches wrecked sex shops. But in Ireland, the stakes were high: "mothers for peace" set up an organization in 1976 to protest terrorist killings, while in Chile, women relatives of men who had "disappeared" under the repressive regime, organized silent demonstrations each day, starting in 1977.

Women, it appeared, were at two major turning points of humanity: the oldest human skeleton, discovered in 1974 in the Afar desert of Ethiopia, was that of a woman. She was dubbed Lucy, the "mother of humanity". And the first test-tube baby was also female. She was born in London in 1978 and named Louise Brown. Nothing would ever be the same again.

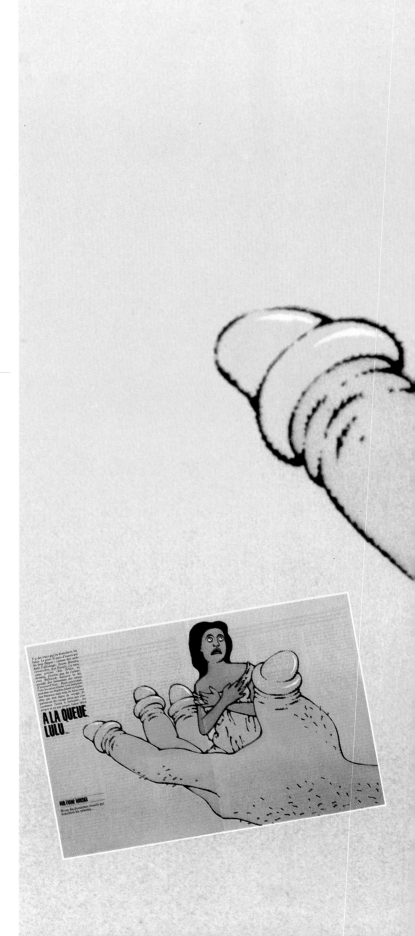

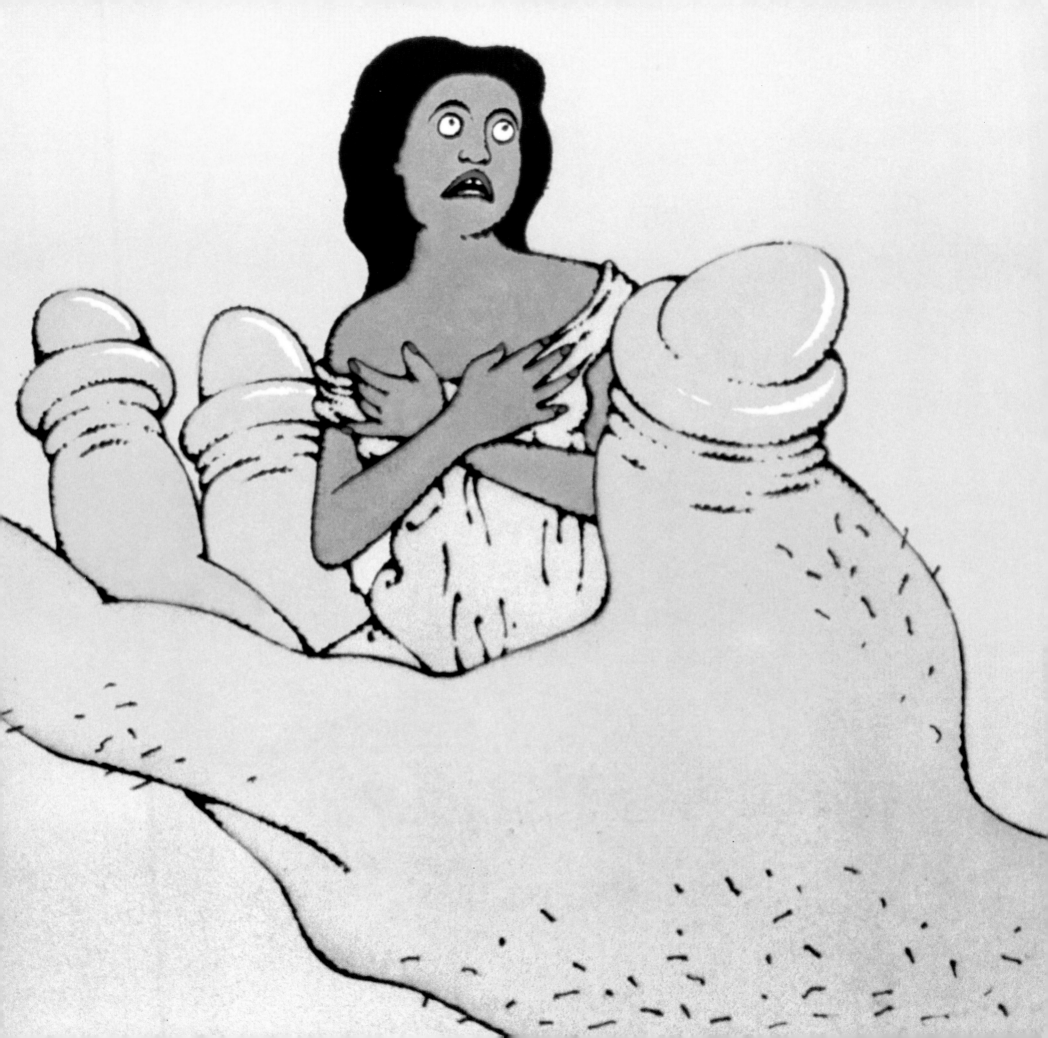

Liz Bijl
Firestone tire calendar for truck drivers, 1973.

Bob Lawrie
NTA, 1975.

Meier Baum
Cover of Actuel no. 4, 1969. "Down with Male-dominated Society".

Guy Ferry
Cover design
for Zoom
(France),
1972

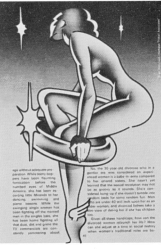

Bush Hollyhead
Sunday Times (London),
1975.

Bob Lawrie
NTA, 1973.

Miriam Wosk
"Jewish
American
Princess".
Unpublished
cover design
for New
Woman,
1971.

Willardsey
Cover of West
(USA),
February 1972.

Miriam Wosk
Cover for
Ms. Magazine
for its fifth
anniversary,
1977.

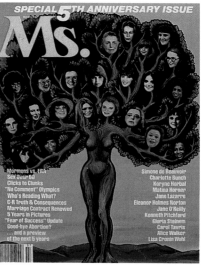

Miriam Wosk
Cover for
Ms. Magazine,
no. 1, 1972.

**Andresjz
Dudzinski**
Cover of
Ty i ja
(Poland),
1973.

Hedda Johnson

Push Pin Graphic, no. 56, 1967. "Woman and religion" and "Woman and money".

Paul Davis

Esquire, 1967.

Milton Glaser
Ramparts.
"Abortion".

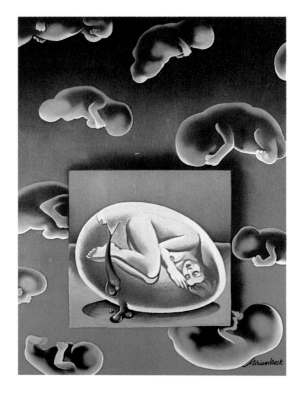

Miriam Wosk
Ms. Magazine,
1972.
"Abortion".

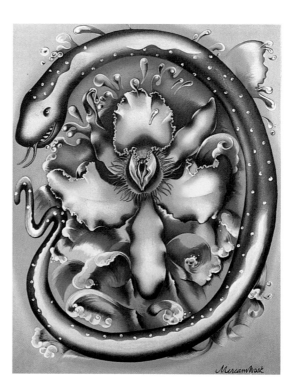

Miriam Wosk
Ms. Magazine,
1972.
"The liberated
orgasm".

68

Barbara Nessim
Viva Magazine, 1974.
"Grass roots women power".

Barbara Nessim
Ms. Magazine, 1972.
"Women and madness".

Virginie Thévenet
Cree (France),
April-May 1973.
"Les groupies
du président Mao",
on President Mao's
groupies.

Virginie Thévenet
Cree (France),
April-May 1973.
"Le détachement
féminin rouge",
on Chinese women
under arms.

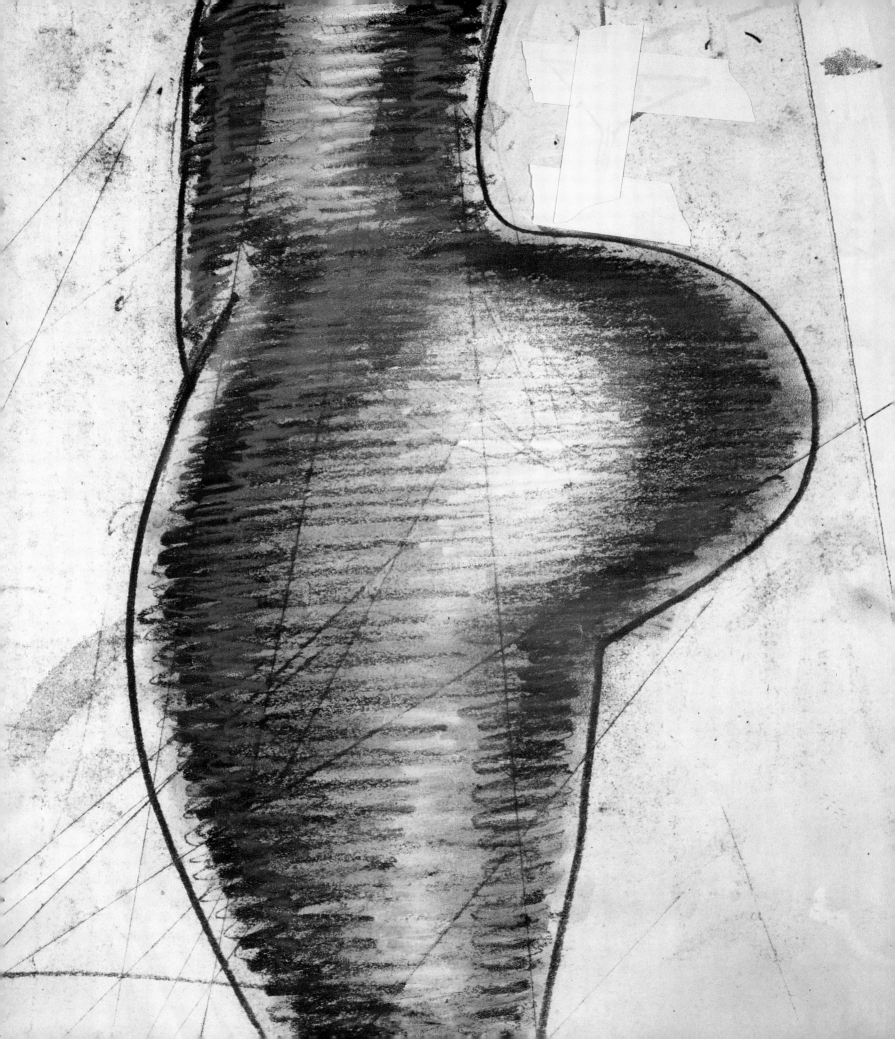

Patrick Arlet
Playboy France, 1979.
"Les forçats du culturisme" or men's addiction to body-building.

Men On the Defensive

Confronted with feminists on the march, most men tried to keep an amused smile on their face. They could not and did not want to believe what they were seeing.

Machos alive and kicking! This was not a battle cry, but merely a daily fact of life. It was a widespread sentiment expressed in different ways, and notably through pictures. The "twins" of French magazine illustration, Alain Le Saux and Philippe Corentin, excelled at rendering masculine attitudes, especially as they were working for a monthly called Lui, dubbed "the magazine for modern men." Their illustrations, however, were quite deceptive. A close look reveals that they were in fact highly critical of the prevalent coercive masculine attitudes. Their weapons were unrelenting anger and scathing humour.

Once macho attitudes were seriously shaken, men became sexist. The psychological distinction is important: whereas the former is on the offensive, taking an exaggeratedly strong stand to prove he is a real he-man, the latter is on the defensive, full of spite, reactionary and totalitarian in spirit. In Latin American, women are in the habit of saying, "There's nothing worse than a sexist male, but nothing better than a macho male."

Unfortunately, sexist men take an active dislike to women who are free, and particularly liberated women. Even more unfortunate, they are much more numerous than machos, which is why the feminist fight encountered such tremendous resistance.

The hottest issue centred on the sexual freedom of women. It was relatively easy for men to accept the success stories of Indira Gandhi, Marguerite Yourcenar, Golda Meir or Valentina Terechkowa, who took on essentially masculine roles and became symbols of what women could do. Sexual freedom was an entirely different matter. Women showed the most combativity and inventiveness in the areas of contraception and abortion. Men, meanwhile, were in a holding operation of virile domination.

Le Saux and Corentin used a revolver and holster to symbolize this virile hostility. Men with their paraphenalia pretended to be hot shots! They tried to keep their chins up, but it wasn't easy, for women were hitting below the belt.

In the sexist camp, it was the beginning of a masculine retreat, as Corentin's drawing illustrates so well (see page 81). But that was only the beginning.

The future did not look bright, and men were about to become not the dominant but the dominated sex. More and more women took an anti-male stand. The drawing by Bush Hollyhead of a tube of

Alain Le Saux
Jasmin (Germany), 1972.
"Wie ich mein auto liebe?…".
Article on the ambiguous relationship men have with their cars.

Patrick Arlet
Playboy Germany,
1984.
Illustration for a short
story by Charles
Bukowski.

toothpaste being squashed with fury and contempt by a high heel couldn't be more explicit (see page 82). This was about the time that homosexual demands for freedom became strident.

What had started out as a retreat became a rout. In the end, men preferred to take their walking papers. They had not expected to be overrun with such tremendous force, and it caught them totally unprepared. The traditional image of women fell to pieces, as did former practices of exploiting that image. Playboy clubs began to lose attendance, and men increasingly resorted to more and more degrading representations of women, making clandestine visits to sex shops, which saw an unprecedented era of prosperity before peep shows made inroads into that market.

In short, forms of solitary pleasure-seeking that are usually associated with pre-adolescence became appropriate for all age groups.

Following the lead of their female counterparts, male homosexuals began staking out their own claims. The phenomenon did not escape the sharp eye of magazine illustrators. The at once dreamlike and crude Patrick Arlet, and Roman Cieslewicz, with his scathing collages, each drove home the point in his own fashion. A few generations back, the poet Aragon had called "woman the future of man". Should his line have been changed to "man is the future of man"?

It was a strange period that saw the end of old fixations and the beginning of pluralistic forms of pleasure. But it also saw the disappearance of rites and ritual whose absence leaves a huge gap. Courtship was turned into an insult. In any "revolution", of course, excesses are always committed. In this instance, sexuality was turned into something that came close to being a consumer product.

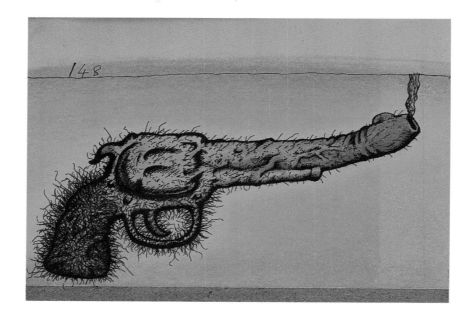

Philippe Corentin
Lui, no. 202,
November 1980.
"Porcs d'armes",
or the close relation-
ship between guns
and male sexists.

Alain Le Saux
Lui, no. 75,
April 1970.
"West Sex Story",
or conquering
the West.

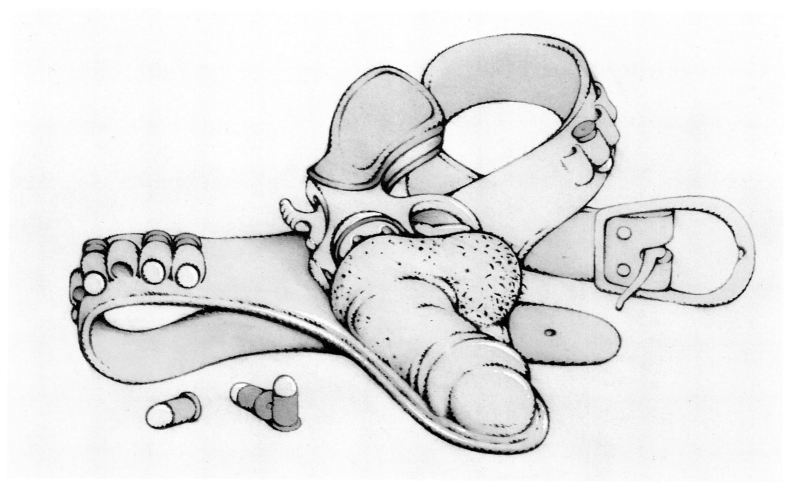

Alain Le Saux
Lui, no. 249,
October 1984.
"Mateur
dolorosa",
or the rise of
pornographic
films.

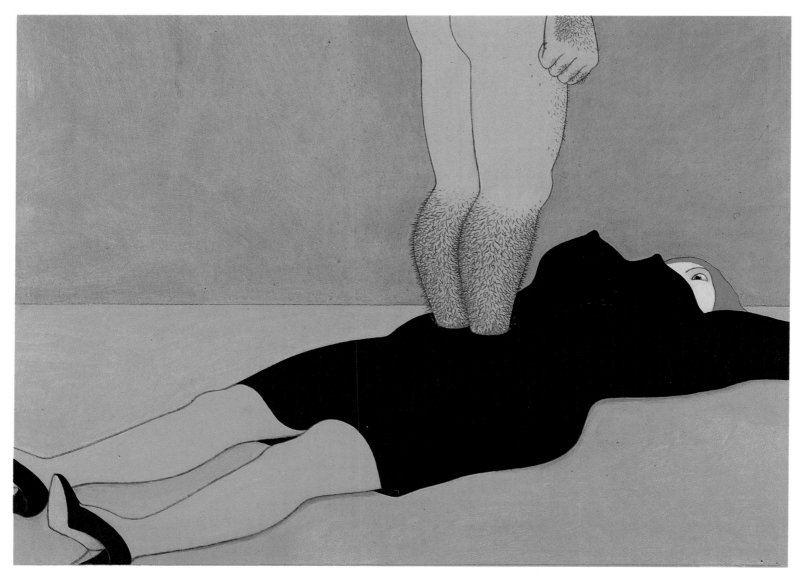

Alain Le Saux
Lui, no. 194, March 1980. "Gens d'âmes et violeurs", article on rape in the United States.

French editorial illustrators typically took a strong concept and played it for what it was worth. Here, Le Saux positions two bodies in almost identical fashion, yet each drawing takes on a completely different meaning.

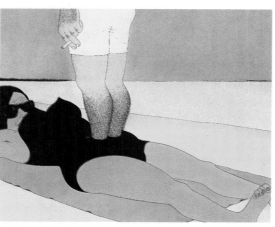

Alain Le Saux
Lui, no. 183, April 1979. "Bureaux des cœurs", or the fad for personal ads.

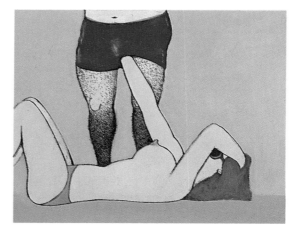

Alain Le Saux
Lui, no. 195, April 1980. "Mimiles et une nuits" or how women pick up men.

Alain Le Saux
Subjectif, 1979.

Alain Le Saux
Lui, no. 211,
August 1981.
"Sympa… trique".

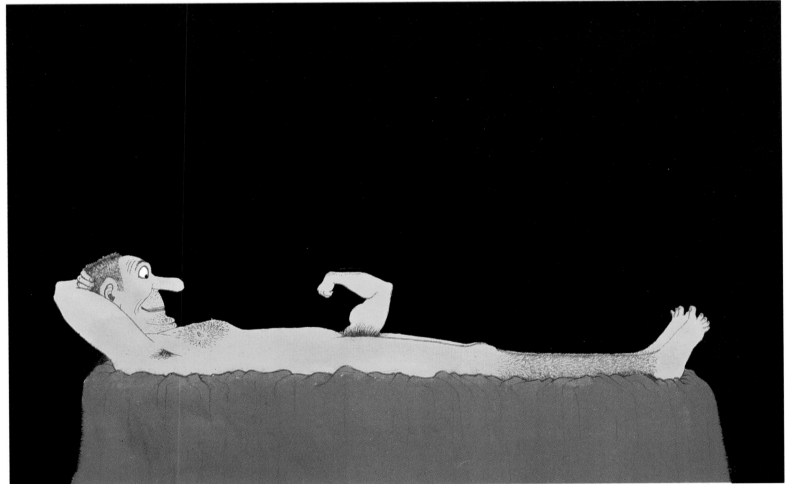

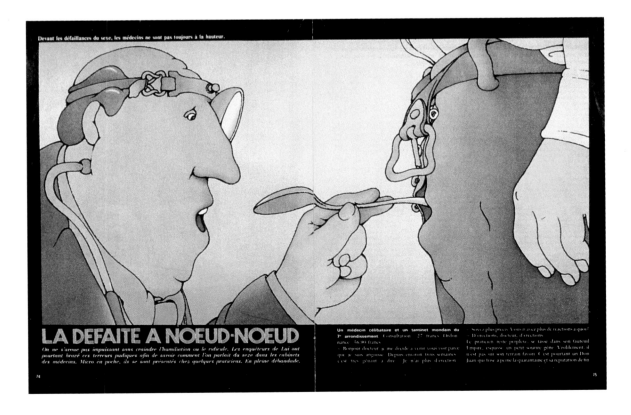

Bush Hollyhead
NTA, 1975.

Patrick Arlet
Lui, no. 175,
August 1978.
"Les tantes de
l'oncle Tom",
article
on the rites
and hangouts
of male homo-
sexuals.

**Roman
Cieslewicz**
"Gâteux
au bas Dim".
Collage, 1976.

Jean Lagarrigue
Esquire, 1969 and Lui no. 104, September 1972. "Neighbours", a short story by Raymond Carver, called "Entre vous" when it appeared in the French magazine Lui.

Revolving Couples

Women, men, couples… Opinions on how to live as a couple, as well as ways of living together changed at the same pace as that of other activities, speeding up, slowing down, jerking out of control or brought under control at a pace that no one could predict or understand.

To feel and fathom what was happening or to have a presentiment of what was going to happen, all one had to do was go to the cinema. Here, too, time seemed to speed up or slow down in an unvoidable, symptomatic fashion.

In 1961, two films, François Truffaut's "Jules and Jim" and Stanley Kubrick's "Lolita" explored other ways of living as a couple. The basic lesson that can be drawn from them, however, is that nothing really changes, except the way we experience and express things. By comparison, the film that won the prize at the Cannes Film Festival in 1966—- "Un Homme et Une Femme" by Claude Lelouch—-looked really old hat. The contrast was even more striking once the mini-liberations, utopian dreams and verbiage produced by the student revolt of May 1968 got under way.

Anything and everything seemed to have an impact on the way people lived together as a couple, from the miniskirt to the pill, psychoanalysis, travel, the social sciences, the discovery of primitive societies, and economic affluence. Depending upon their mood or whim, couples formed or split up, while the number of couples contracting marriage dropped noticeably. Freedom, of course, did not exclude jealousy, and curiosity was not much of an excuse in the face of a partner's possessiveness. Quarrels that had been carefully hidden from friends and acquaintances suddenly became topics of conversation.

The nineteenth-century definition of the couple no longer pertained. Other attitudes, this time based on "choice",

became prevalent. The more acceptable term "single mothers" gradually replaced the derogatory "unwed mothers" of the past.

All types of couples, from the more or less traditional to the "non-couple", coexisted, which led to diametrically opposed experiences. In 1969, for example, the first International Sex Fair was held in Copenhagen, while in Paris, Guy Hocquenghem and a handful of friends founded the Front Homosexuel d'Action Révolutionnaire (Homosexual Front for Revolutionary Action). An activist group of transvestites called "Les Gazolines" came out of hiding and lent animation to certain quarters of Paris from dusk till dawn. They quickly moved from spontaneous happenings to the stage of a Paris theatre. All forms of sexuality would soon have a right to a place in the sun.

Film-makers were among those who explored the new forms of sexuality, and even the titles are enough to give some idea of the changing mores. For example, a slew of films was produced in 1972, the most significant being "Nous Ne Vieillirons Pas Ensemble" ("We Won't Grow Old Together") by Maurice Pialat; "L'Amour L'après midi" ("Love in the Afternoon") by Eric Rohmer; "All You Wanted to Know About Sex and Never Dared To Ask" by Woody Allen; "Last Tango in Paris" by Bernardo Bertolucci, "Heat" by Paul Morissey, and "Canterbury Tales" by Pier Paolo Pasolini. These were followed by Bertrand Blier's "Les Valseuses" and "La Maman et la Putain" ("Mama and the Prostitute") by Jean Eustache. Once again, film-makers were expert at sensing which way the wind was blowing, as they captured on film the changes in mores that were taking place.

Even so, the breaking down of old taboos and the exploration of new frontiers did not really bring about deep-

Paul Davis
Cover of New York Magazine, January 1969. "Bachelor Mothers", on the phenomenon of single mothers.

seated changes in the man-woman relationship. In July 1977, a huge brown-out brought the city of New York to a standstill for twenty-four hours. The result was apparent exactly nine months later, as an unprecedented baby boom hit the city!

In 1978, films treated more enduring themes of love: "L'Homme Qui Aimait les Femmes" ("The Man Who Loved Women") by François Truffaut; "Three Women" by Robert Altman, "Annie Hall" by Woody Allen and "The Marriage of Maria Braun" by Rainer Werner Fassbinder.

The world thus seemed to be coming to its senses, but the publication in 1979 of the first issue of Gay Pied (a play on words signifying Gay Pleasure) was like a bugle call. Life, it seemed to say, had not come to a standstill; many changes were still taking place. A large number of sexual partners appeared to be the order of the day, but this led many ordinary people to become increasingly reticent. More and more women found themselves alone, as men threw in the towel. Voyeurism, an unfortunate consequence of an image-oriented society, was on the upswing, at a pace that reflected the ambient avidity of a consumer society. Peep shows were in vogue. Then the spread of AIDS forced men and women to resort to condoms and a careful selection of partners.

It was in the early Eighties that Steven Spielberg started work on a big-budget film that was turned into a fairy tale for modern men and women. The "hero" was a weird, touching and totally sexless creature called "E.T.".

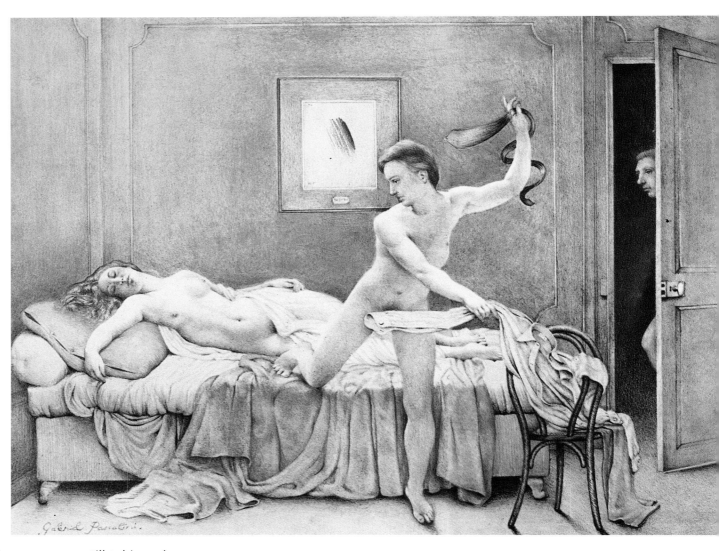

Gabriel Pascalini
Lui, no. 85, February 1971. "Retour à la terre",
a story by Joyce Carol Oates on a young, innocent
girl and two bad boys.

Jean Lagarrigue
Lui, no. 126, July 1974.
"Le guide discret
de la bourgeoisie",
a list of addresses of comfortable
hotels and inns off the beaten track.

Bob Lawrie
NTA, 1972.
"Hands of honey".

Seymour Chwast
"Fred and Rosalie", 1970.

Tadanori Yokoo
1965.

Bob Lawrie
NTA, 1972.
"Dancing Couple".

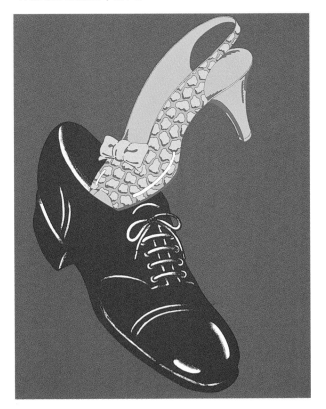

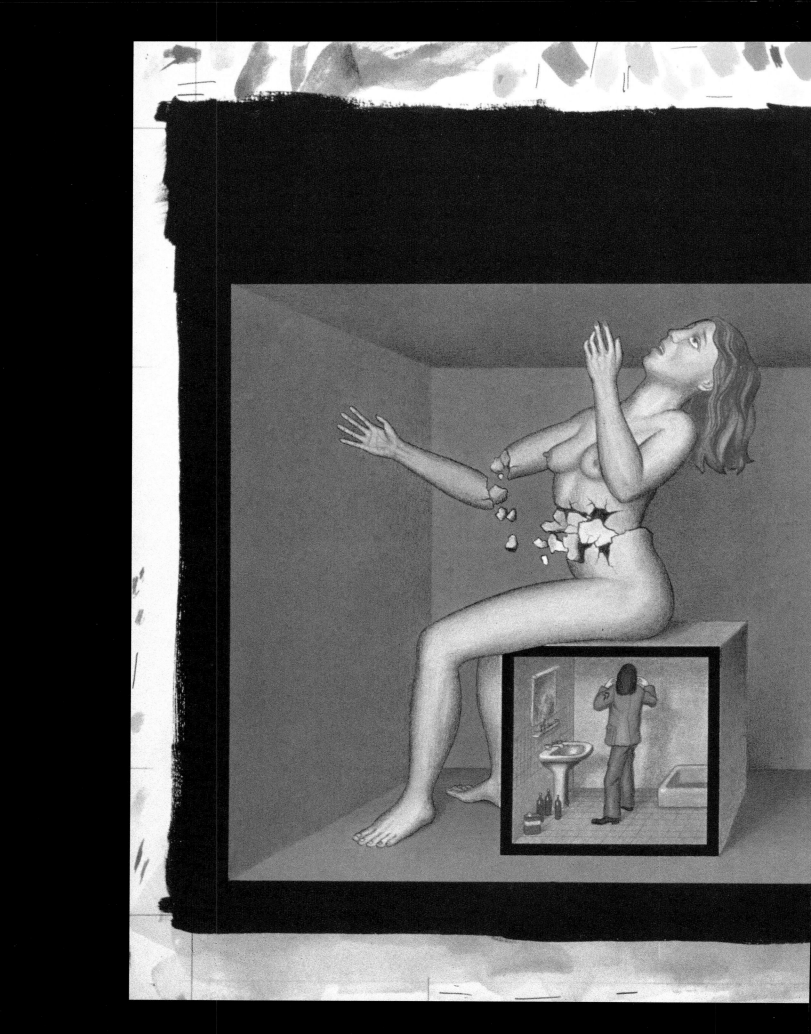

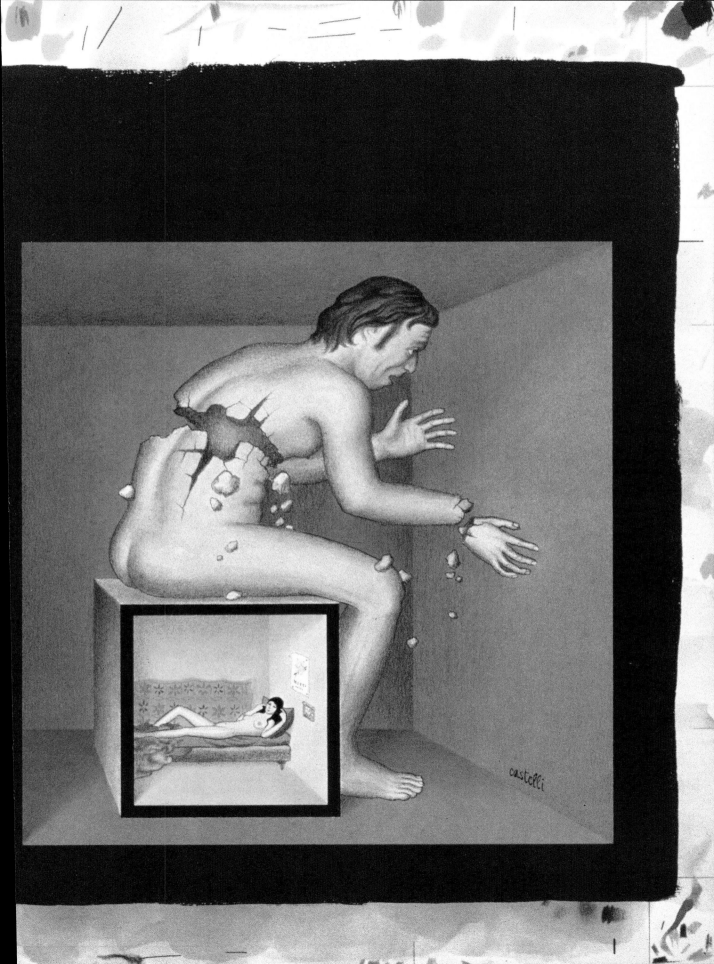

Previous page

Jean-Claude Castelli
Lui, no. 103, august 1972.
"Enragés volontaires", illustration for
a short story by Bertrand Poirot-Delpech.

Jean-Paul Goude
Sketch for "Angel", a film
that was never made.
New York, 1977.

Guy Ferry
1972.

Roman Cieslewicz
"Changements de climat"
or changes of climate.
Collage, 1976.

Barbara Nessim
a personnal work,
1977.

Tadanori Yokoo
1965.

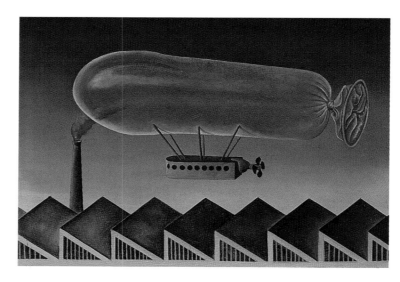

Jean Lagarrigue
Lui, 1973.
"Des marks par
la bande", article
on Beate Uhse,
the queen of West
German sex shops.

Seymour Chwast
"Peridot".
Poster for a video
film company,
1975.

PEEP-SHOW

CURTAIN
25 $ A MINUTE.

CURTAIN
25 $ A MINUTE.

Following page

**Jean-Paul
Goude**
"Peep-show".
Esquisse,
New York, 1977.

Paul Davis
Portrait of Ralph
Nader on a paper
bag, unpublished
cover design for
Time, 1968.

Combatting the World's Ills

It was in California that things were happening. In Los Angeles, America's traditional values and virtues were being brought up to date and put to music by the Beach Boys. San Francisco saw the rise of licentiousness, LSD and long hair, in protest against the three K's (as in Ku Klux Klan) of Amerikkka, the protest being led by such "far out" types as Timothy Leary and Jerry Rubin.

But out of the clear blue sky came a new kind of crusader (who served as an inspiration for the Blues Brothers a few years later). Stirring up a great fuss in Washington, D.C., in 1966, Ralph Nader publicly questioned the safety of the Corvair aircraft. In so doing, he invented the notion of consumer protection, creating a new type of lobby comprised of deceived, cheated and exploited consumers. At the time, Nader was a thirty-one-year-old lawyer. He has devoted his lifetime to defending his ideas, and in the past thirty-odd years, he has seen them triumph. People everywhere have copied his Center for the Study of Responsive Law or Public Citizen, which he founded respectively in 1966 and 1971. He was amazingly efficacious: from 1966 to 1973, he pressured Congress into passing twenty-five reform bills.

Nader was a trail blazer. But there were others like him, who had not succumbed to the fascination with affluence or submitted to the temptations of the consumer society. Among the French writers who sounded the alarm were Georges Perec in "Les Choses" (or "Things", 1965) and Jean Baudrillard in "Le Système des Objets" ("The System of Objects", 1968) and "La Société de Consommation" ("The Consumer Society", 1970). A number of illustrators also saw danger lurking, among them,

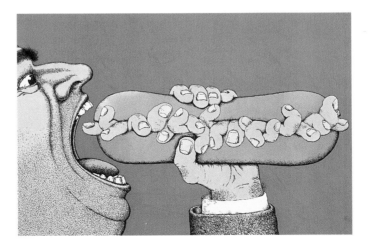

Arlet (page 99), Cieslewicz (page 98) and Le Saux (see this page). Their message was relayed by Marco Ferreri in 1973 with his film "La Grande Bouffe" (which roughly translates as "The Great Gorging"). In 1975, painters Cueco, Fleury, Parré and Tisserand banded together in the Coopérative des Malassis to paint a fresco covering the two-thousand-square-meter façade of a shopping centre in the outskirts of Grenoble. Called "Le Radeau de la Méduse", after Géricault's famous painting, it showed the consumer society adrift. While half of humanity starved to death, the other half gorged itself. This was the "throwaway" society: in 1975, the first disposable razors epitomized the general attitude towards belongings. They were bought quickly, consumed quickly, thrown away quickly and forgotten quickly.

The oil price-hikes of 1973 and 1976 were a rude shock to the West. Though they did not institute a reversal of trends, they did incite the West to practise greater economic rigour. Following hard on the heels of consumerism, environmental concerns became a new rallying cry. Pollution and ecology gradually became catch words, then became accepted, everyday terms.

On March 18, 1967, the Torrey Canyon tanker spilled a horrendous blanket of oil onto the coast of Brittany. It was terribly shocking, but was nonetheless considered an accident. Eleven years later, on March 16, 1978, the Amoco Cadiz spilled eighty thousand tons of oil on the Brittany coast. This time the spill was no longer called an "accident". Rather, the captain of the tanker was accused of committing a "pollution offence".

Among other shocking pollution cases was the extremely

Alain Le Saux
Lui, no. 128, September 1974. "Croque-monsieur".

grave accident at Seveso, Italy, on July 20, 1976, during which a cloud of poisonous dioxine gas spread for miles. Another scary accident was at the Three Mile Island nuclear plant in Pennsylvania on March 28, 1979, that released radioactive particles into the air. It gave a slight idea of what a nuclear disaster like Tchernobyl could be. Generally speaking, governments tried to gloss over the incidents, to hush things up, for the economic stakes were too high. And yet little by little and in dispersed fashion, citizens began to organize. In France, a fire in a dance hall at Saint-Laurent du Pont in November 1970 killed one hundred and forty-six adolescents. Public indignation ran so high that it forced the authorities to take more stringent safety measures. In fact, France became the country with the most draconian regulations for public places.

In April 1972, six thousand people on bicycles crossed Paris in a protest for clean air. It served to draw public attention to carbon dioxide exhaust fumes. In 1973, twenty-one children were killed in a fire that was one among many hastily built schools. This lead to an overhaul of regulations concerning prefabricated buildings.

It obviously took a serious accident, an ecological catastrophe or a personal tragedy to force legislators to take action. A number of ecological groups saw the light of day in Italy, Japan, Germany and the United States. In France, in 1974, an exhibition called "Les Energies Libres" ("Free Energies ") was organized at the Musée des Arts Décoratifs; the poster was designed by Reiser, active in an ecology publication called La Gueule Ouverte.

In 1975, the then Minister of Health Simone Veil launched the first campaign against cigarette smoking, similar to the one undertaken in the United States. On either side of the Atlantic Ocean, the bards of anti-smoking were two of the mainstays of Push Pin Studios, Seymour Chwast and Milton Glaser. In 1976, Jean-Michel Jarre, of synthetiser fame, found himself at the top of the international hit parade with an album entitled "Oxygen".

It was not until the French municipal elections held in March 1977 that the names of the first "green" candidates were to be found in polling booths. Though these early environmentalists did not meet with electoral success, they had at least got themselves a speaker's platform. The following August, all the environmental organizations, many of whose members were former leftists, joined together to protest the extension of military installations on the Larzac plateau in southwestern France. In the first of a series of demonstrations, several hundred people shouted that the area should be preserved for shepherds. On several occasions, they had to contend with squads of riot police, and Larzac became associated in people's minds with the fight to preserve unspoiled landscapes.

In short, environmentalism had been launched. Preserving the countryside was not the sole concern. Adepts soon turned their attention to the multifarious health hazards and threats to the quality of life that pertained in modern cities.

The fall-out of the May 1968 revolts was revealing. Citizens were losing faith in politicians' politics. Former extreme left-wingers who sung the praises of liberating utopias were converting to new beliefs. Environmentalism held out new hope, just as humanitarian action was opening up new vistas.

Amnesty International was founded in October 1962 by Peter Benenson and Sean MacBride. For years, it was an obscure movement, but it finally came into the glare of international spotlights. In December 1973, Amnesty organized an international meeting to abolish torture. The subject was so timely and affected so many countries that the meeting drew international recognition. From that point on, Amnesty International became a respected, and even feared, voice. It then undertook even broader actions and commitments, so much so that on December 20, 1977, Amnesty International, as a non-government organization, was awarded the Nobel Peace Prize.

Other forms of humanitarian action were also taking place. During the months of August and September 1968, Nigeria was the scene of genocide. The Ibos, who inhabited Biafra, were savagely and systematically massacred. A young French doctor by the name of Bernard Kouchner worked tirelessly bandaging, operating on and amputating the wounded. Horrified by the extent of the massacre

Jean Lagarrigue
Lui, no. 111, April 1973.
"Les restes de l'oncle
Sam", at the end of
the Vietnam war.

Patrick Arlet
Playboy France, 1980.
"Les marées noires",
on oil pollution.

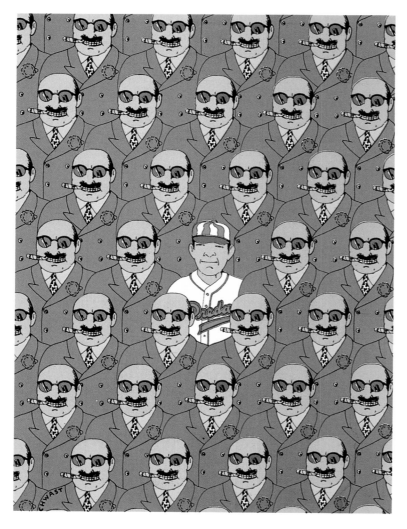

Seymour Chwast
Three posters against
smoking, 1966/1967.

Milton Glaser
"Smoking pollutes".
Poster, 1967.

and helpless in the face of so much suffering, he dreamed up the concept of "humanitarian intervention".

In December 1971, Bernard Kouchner, joined by a handful of doctor friends, including Rony Braumann, Hervé Emmanuelli and Claude Malhuret, founded "Médecins Sans Frontières" (Doctors Without Borders). The "French Doctors" legend was born, and was reinforced by the founding of "Médecins du Monde" (Doctors of the World) in 1980. Next came such other organizations as Action Internationale Contre La Faim (International Action Against Hunger) and, some years later, SOS Racism. Still others grouped nurses, reporters and pharmacists. Much later, there were even musicians: in 1985, led by Irish singer Bob Geldof, a gigantic audience attended the first "live aid" concert to help the Ethiopians who were starving to death. The concert was televised and broadcast to one hundred and forty countries, reaching an audience of one and a half billion viewers. Some eight and a half million dollars was collected.

"Charity business" was born in Wembley, and it soon was going strong. In 1979, leading philosophers Jean-Paul Sartre, Raymond Aron, Michel Foucault and André Glucksman met with the French President. Thanks to their plea, a ship called "L'Ile de la Lumière" was armed with supplies and sent to the China Sea to help the Vietnamese boat people. Faced with the disasters of war, torture, dictatorship, and natural disasters, ordinary individuals—-and not governments or international organizations—-rose to the challenge. Millions of individuals proudly bore the standard of great causes and even won some victories.

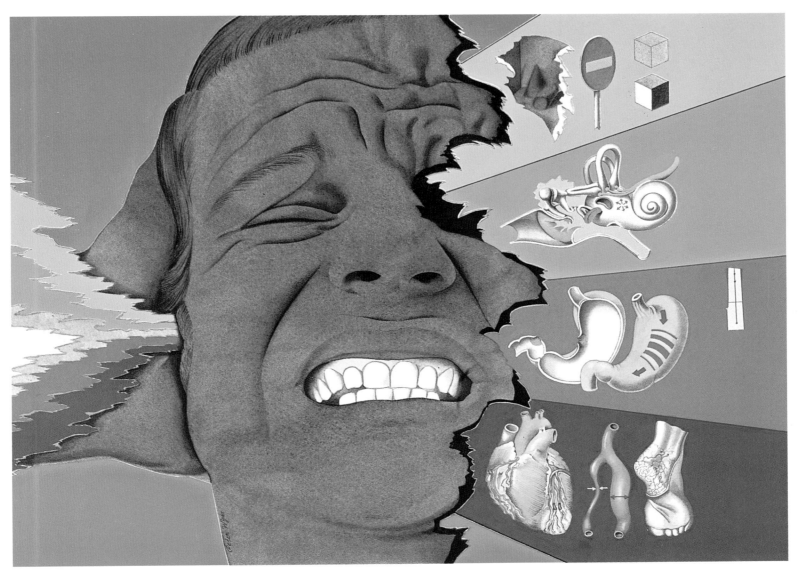

Peter Wyss

Illustration for a
health book,
Editions Sauret.

"Fresh Air Fiends"
Push Pin Graphic, no.
54, 1966.

Milton Glaser
"Don't Eat Grapes". Poster in support of grape pickers, 1972.

Milton Glaser
"You Are What You Eat". Poster for a film that was never shot, 1967.

Philippe Corentin
Lui, no. 167, December 1977. "En vert et contre tout", on preserving the environment.

François de Constantin
Okapi, children's magazine, 1978.

Roland Topor
"Help". Poster for a Unesco campaign, 1982.

André François
"La tête fleurie". 1966. This small character was frequently used by publisher Robert Delpire for over thirty years on letterheads and for other editorial purposes.

Shigeo Fukuda
"Environmental Pollution".
Poster, 1973.

Avoine
Poster devoted to urban policy for
the French Socialist Party's first
European election campaign. 1979.

George Hardie
Sunday Times, 1977.
"The Blind
Mechanic".

Jean-Claude Castelli
Poster for an interna-
tional competition
to build a centre at
Les Halles in Paris,
launched by architect
Jean Nouvel in
reaction to govern-
ment projects.
February 1980.

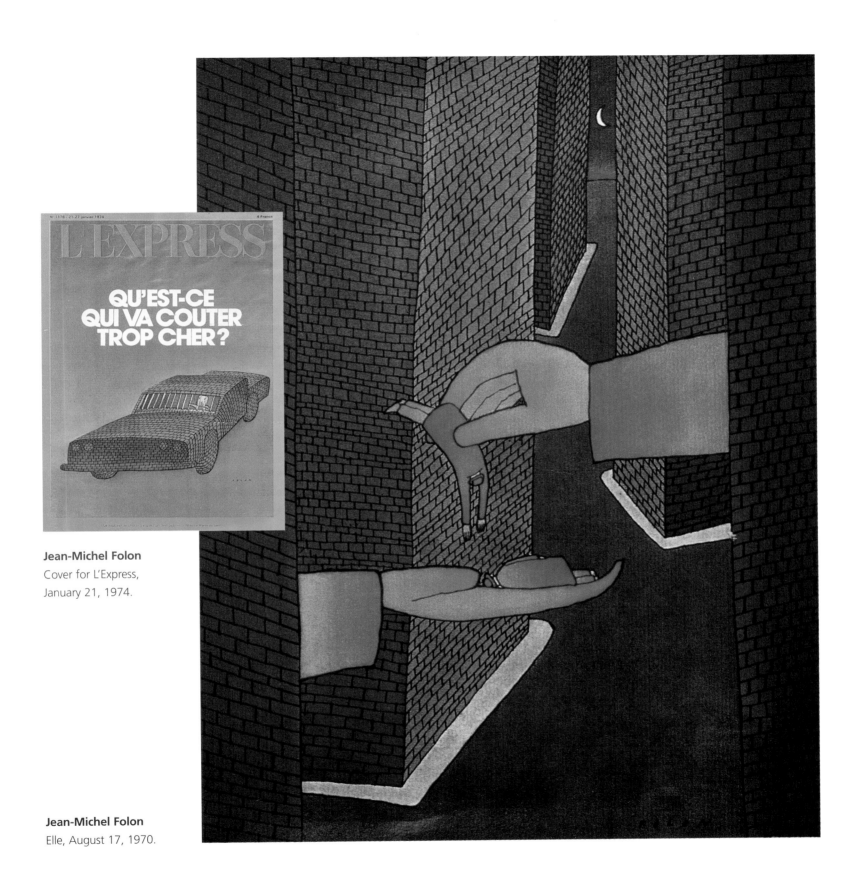

Jean-Michel Folon
Cover for L'Express,
January 21, 1974.

Jean-Michel Folon
Elle, August 17, 1970.

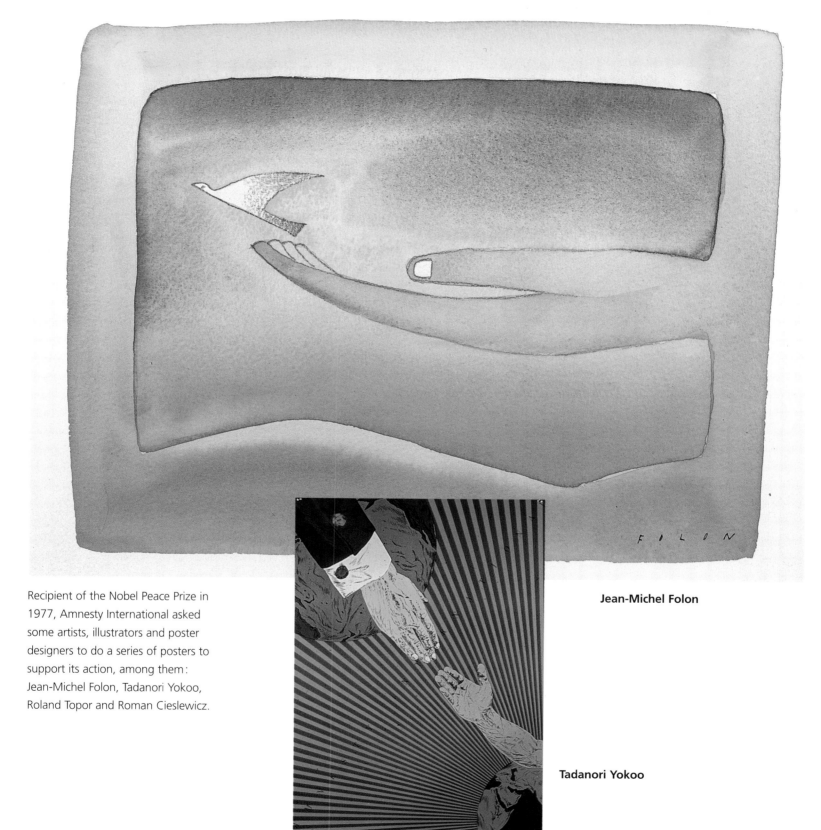

Jean-Michel Folon

Recipient of the Nobel Peace Prize in 1977, Amnesty International asked some artists, illustrators and poster designers to do a series of posters to support its action, among them: Jean-Michel Folon, Tadanori Yokoo, Roland Topor and Roman Cieslewicz.

Tadanori Yokoo

Roland Topor

Roman Cieslewicz
"Corps diplomatique", poster to combat neo-colonialism and hunger in the world, 1974.

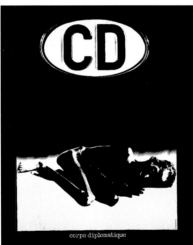

Shigeo Fukuda
"Decade for Action", poster to fight against racism, 1977.

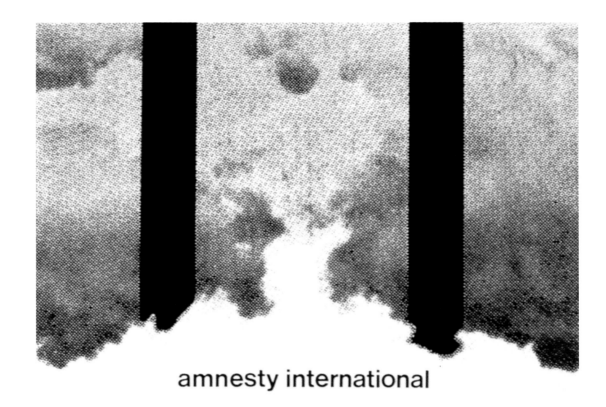

amnesty international

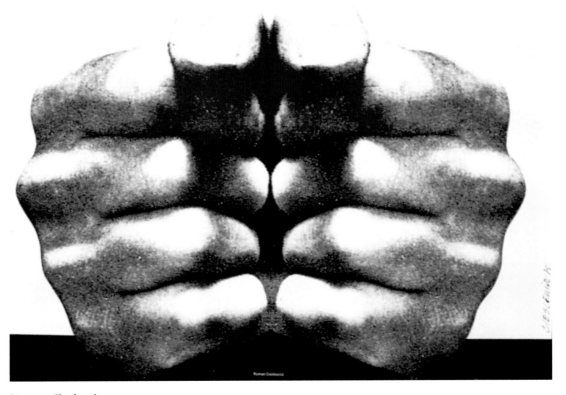

Roman Cieslewicz

Jean Lagarrigue
Esquire,
September 1968.
"Psychoanalysis
Must Go".

Existential Angst

An amusing Jewish anecdote goes like this: "For Jesus, everything is love; for Marx, everything is economics; for Freud, everything is sex; and for Einstein, everything is relative." During the Sixties and Seventies, people found Jesus somewhat irrelevant, Marx somewhat out of fashion and Einstein somewhat too subtle.

Another Jewish joke asks the question, "What is the difference between a tailor and a psychoanalyst?" The answer: "A generation". Across the United States, and especially in New York, pyschoanalysis was all the fashion. Everyone who was anyone was in analysis, and it was considered a very serious business, even if psychoanalysts were jokingly referred to as "shrinks". Be that as it may, this was the heyday of Freud.

In Paris, a star was born that was to shed light on the entire Western world. In 1964, Jacques Lacan founded the French Freudian school, attracting the cream of the Parisian intelligentsia to its Left Bank location on the Rue de Lille. There was standing room only at the seminar he gave, and his "Ecrits" ("Writings"), published in 1966, became a best-seller, at least for a book of its kind. In addition to a keen interest in psychology, the public, and particularly young people, were attracted to the social sciences, and especially sociology. The corollary was dreams of a perfect society where everyone would be liberated one day, but meanwhile everyone was in revolt against prevailing norms. Day-to-day living was not easy.

That is where Freud and Lacan, Jung and Adorno came in. Later, in 1972, they were joined by Deleuze and Guattari with their anti-Oedipus concept. It was becoming more and more frequent to find people experiencing existential difficulties that they hoped to get rid of. With the growing availability of medical treatment to all levels

FREUD DOPO 40 ANNI

of French society came an unfortunate tendency to hypochondria. And as the media invaded all corners of society, doctors and psychoanalysts made frequent appearances on television. Indeed, they were turned into something akin to media stars, and from then on, the two were joined by the social worker to form a kind of modern Holy Trinity. They were no longer perceived merely as "healers" but as "orientators", i.e., those who could guide one to a better life.

Perhaps one of the most striking examples of this phenomenon was the worldwide admiration for Christian Barnard, the South African surgeon who performed the first human heart transplant on December 3, 1967.

Once again, alienation lay lurking, not far behind liberation, which only made living more difficult than before. Some observers noticed the dangers lurking behind this psychological dependence. Among the illustrators, Castelli's theme was medicine; Lagarrigue's split personalities; Pascalini's the fear of day-to-day existence; and Dudzinski's self-consummation. Magazine pages were filled with this fall into an abyss. In later years, this struck readers as extremely odd, for by then they themselves had become accustomed to magazines giving them advice.

Here, too, illustrators let loose their anger, even if they were lone voices in the wilderness. And when Jean-Luc Godard's "Pierrot Le Fou" brought its explosive message in 1965, audiences didn't get it, because they were more interested in the form.

Generally, people were fascinated with progress yet they suffered from ancestral fears. Everything was suddenly compressed; how could one see clearly, much less reason properly? In 1968, the alarm bell rang again. Stanley Kubrick—-yes, him again—-shook audiences up with his "Space Odyssey 2001", the hero of which was a com-

Roland Topor

Cover for the Corriere della Sera supplement, 1979.

puter. This, for sure, was a major step into modernity. And what modernity! A height was reached at the World Fair in Osaka in 1970, a sort of ode to technology, to economic development, to the conquest of new frontiers and outer space.

Things were getting better...or were they? Reality often contradicted the postulate. Shadow followed light in alternate patterns.

In October 1972, a plane crashed at the top of the Andean cordillera. It proved impossible to locate the wreckage until the month of December. The rescue team finally found some of the passengers, alongside a large number of mutilated bodies. Those who had survived were nearly frozen to death. To stay alive, they had eaten the corpses of their fellow passengers. All sorts of euphemisms were used to describe this unprecedented act of cannibalism, "unprecented" because no one had ever associated Argentinians and Chileans, and therefore members of Western culture, with such an act of barbarism.

About this time, the French artist Jean-Pierre Raynaud dug in, that is, he built himself an underground house, a tile-house, a cenotaph-house. His house became the artist's major work, and he rarely allowed outsiders to enter. He opened it to the public in 1975, only to shut it for twenty years, at which point he finally destoyed it. During that 1975 visit, a journalist wrote an article called "Raynaud, Fear Incarnate."

He was not mistaken. Fear was everywhere, and it only got worse. It was as if the inescapable corollary of ownership in an affluent, not to say opulent society was an overwhelming need for security.

A number of them pointed their finger at this fear (see pages 118-119).

It was not surprising that once psychoanalysts and doctors had breached the wall, quack doctors were quick to follow. What is more, as traditional social structures broke down, and religions and ideologies lost their following, people lost their sense of direction. Given this and the encroachments of television, with its powers of fascination, alienation, and stultification, everything seemed to lead quite naturally to the rapid expansion of religious sects. Indeed,

Di Marco

Cover of
revamped
Actuel,
no. 6,
April 1980.

Les aventures de Jacques Lacan, psychanalyste, page 32

they grew, prospered and multiplied. Society still put them in the same category as hippy communes, just another epiphenomenon of social disorder. The difference was that sects promised hope and not flower-printed shirts, and members chanted in chorus rather than smoking pot as if it were an Indian peace pipe.

Sects were perfectly acceptable until that awful day in September 1978 when nine hundred members of the Temple of the Sun —men, women and even children— committed collective suicide in the Guyana jungle, and this on the instructions of their guru Jim Jones.

The last unfortunate consequence of this endemic difficulty in accepting everyday life was the search for artificial paradises. The gate is narrow between psychoanalysis and sects, and the path filled with tender grasses. Marijuana, then haschich, induced dreams and undid them. The more one smoked, the more one wanted to smoke. Successors were opium and LSD, mescalin and cocain, until heroin and then crack came along. Two Americans were leading the way to paradise. William Burroughs with two hell-bound books: "Junky" and "The Naked Lunch". Then, too, there was Timothy Leary, the apostle of LSD and the author of "The Psychedelic Experience", who was arrested for that very reason in 1966. Leary had two influential friends, however, who presented a powerful defence: Bob Dylan and John Lennon. They were good at proselytizing, and the result was the first love-in, held in San Francisco in October 1966. Some thirty thousand young people gathered together under clouds of incense and haschich, crying "Make love, not war!" From that point on, drugs became a sociological phenomenon.

The market for drugs got structured, and so did repression. The gentle tree of life on which hippies spun sweet dreams was turned into an upward sales spiral. Artificially induced sensations were still there for the having, but heaven had turned to hell.

An avenging angel arose like Saint George killing the dragon. A doctor by the name of Claude Olievenstein was named head of a big hospital in the Paris suburb of Corentin. He set up the first centre to treat drug addicts.

Jean-Claude Castelli

Playboy France,
July 1974.
"Les facultés
du médecin",
on the life-and-
death power
of doctors.

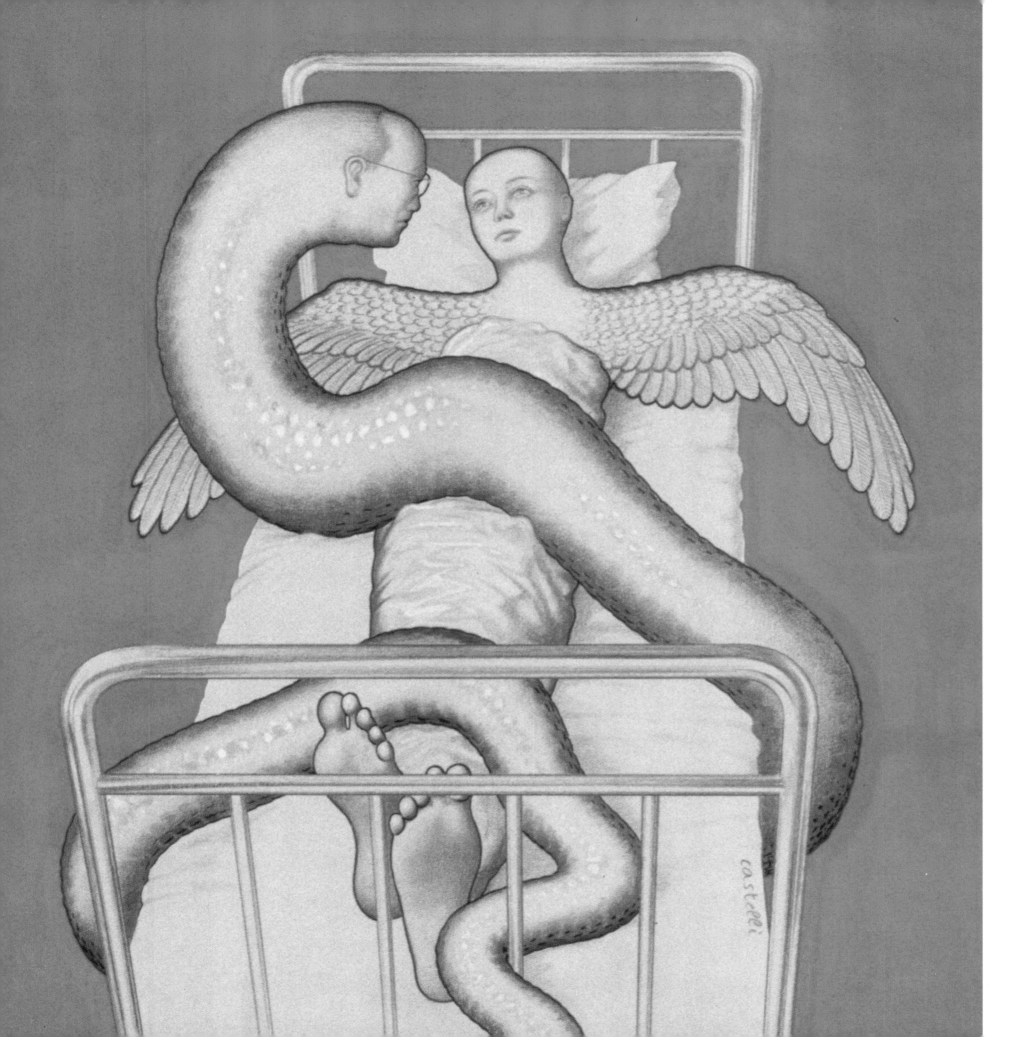

Gabriel Pascalini
Esquire, November 1970.
"Paranoia".

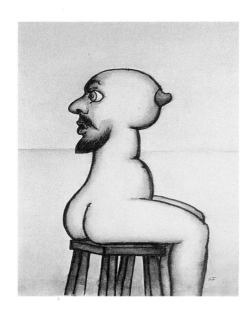

André François
"Dr. Jekyll and Mrs. Freud",
1971.

Jean Lagarrigue
Esquire, 1970.
"The Riddle".

Jean Lagarrigue
Esquire, March 1970.
"Robinson Crusoe
Liebowitz".

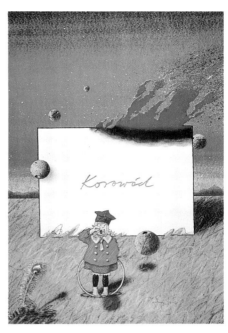

Andresjz Dudzinski
Poster for the film "Kurowod" by Jerzy Karpinski, 1978.

Paul Davis
Show Magazine, 1963.

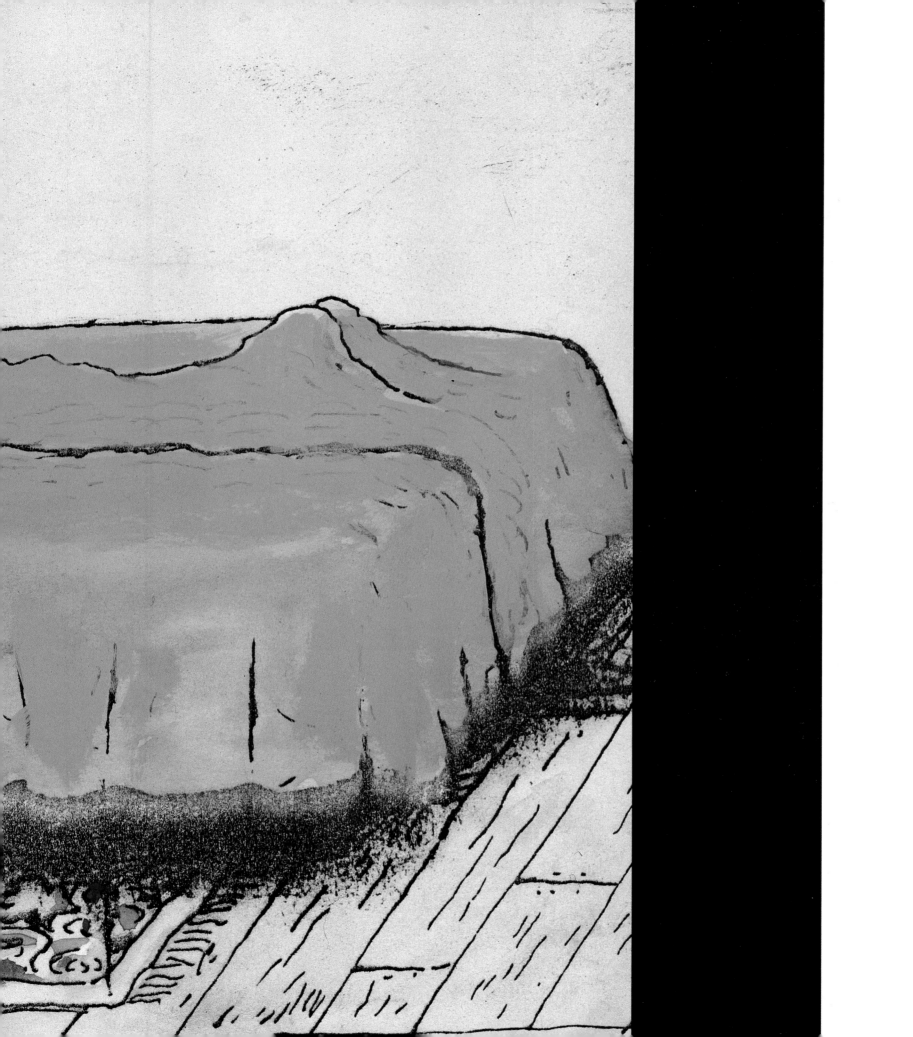

Alain Le Saux
Subjectif, 1979.

Jean Lagarrigue
Lui, no. 216,
January 1982.
"Les revenants
des territoires
d'outre-mort", on
the fear of death.

**Jean-Claude
Castelli**
Unpublished
cover of
L'Express, on
the subject of
"Dumping old
people".

Patrick Arlet
Esquire, 1972.

Alain Le Saux
Lui, no. 198,
July 1980.
"Moscou
ou… moche
coup ?", on
mental torture
in the USSR.

Roland Topor
Cover for
Il Delatore,
1964.

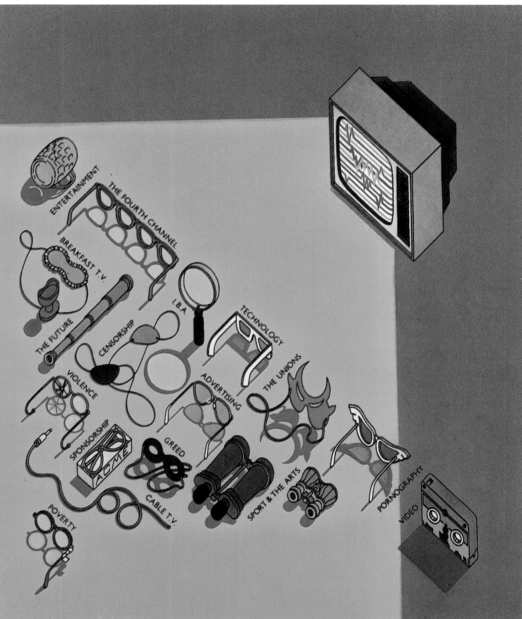

Michel Quarez
La Nouvelle
Critique, 1978.

**Jean-Claude
Castelli**
Lui, no. 81,
October 1970.
"Télé-intox
et masses
médiocres",
or intoxicating TV.

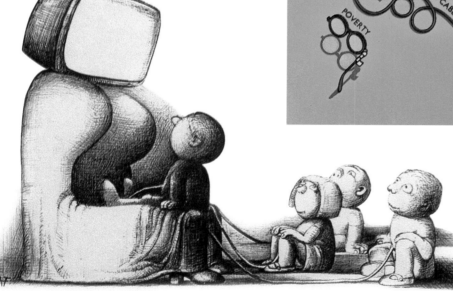

André François
Cover of Le Nouvel Observateur, 1978,
"Télé-dévoreuse", or swallowed by TV.

"Circuit fermé, le bonheur conforme",
or closed circuit conformity, 1978.

Télérama, 1978.
"La télé-nourrice, le cordon ombilical"
or TV umbilical cord.

George Hardie
J'illustre, 1975.

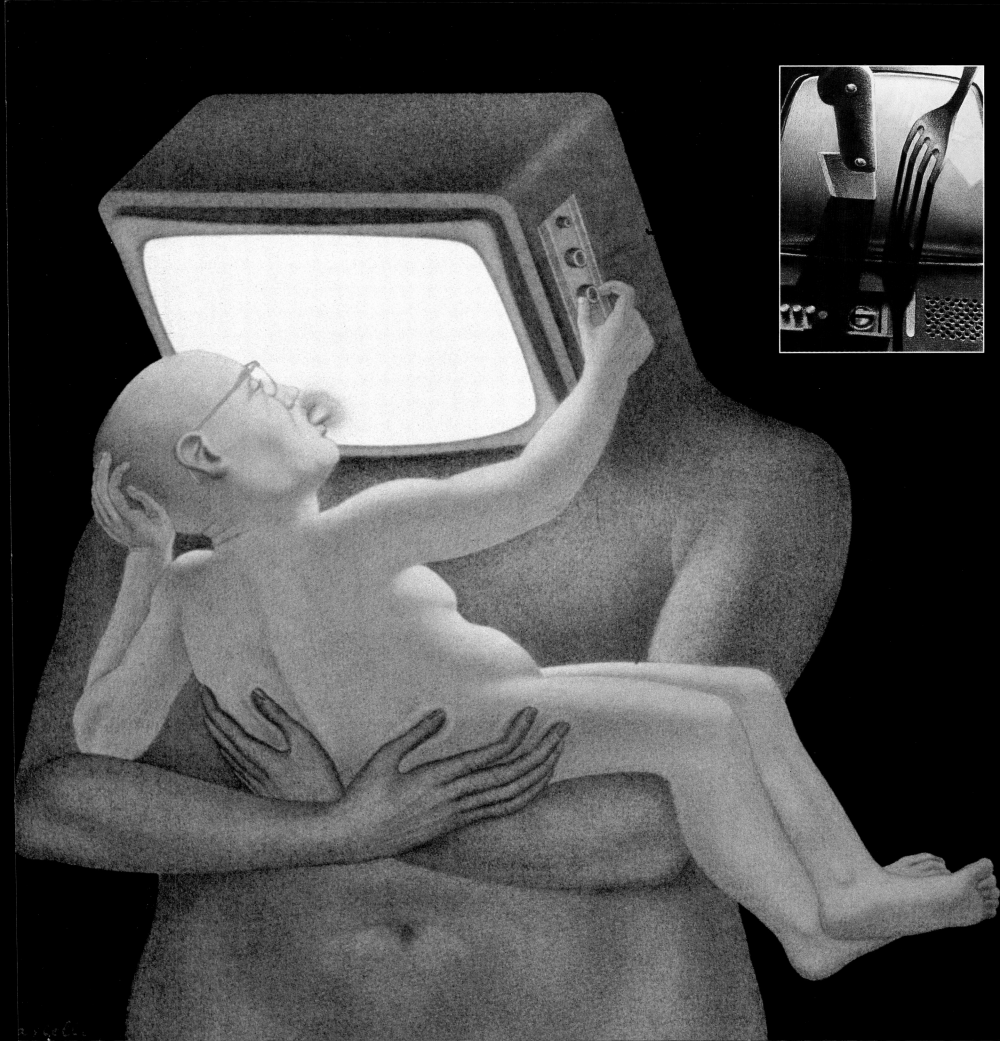

Patrick Arlet
Lui, no. 200,
September
1980.
"Rock Around
The Doc".

Patrick Arlet
Lui, no. 230,
March 1983.
"Haro sur
l'héro", on the
dangerous
drug trade.

Patrick Arlet
Lui, no. 254,
March 1985.
"U.S.A. 1990 :
les latinos
attaquent".

Patrick Arlet
Lui, no. 241,
February 1984.
"E fuma
España !…"

Philippe Corentin
Record, no. 63, May 1976.
Dr. Claude Olievenstein, the first
to help drug addicts, shown as
St. George slaying the dragon.

Jean Lagarrigue
Nova, 1974. "24 Hours
in the Life of a British
Business-woman".

Jean Lagarrigue
Tages Anzeiger (Switzerland),
no. 19, May 1975.
"Lutte contre l'héroïne".

Paul Davis
Portrait of Bob
Dylan.
Cover of
Rolling Stone,
1974.

124

Sex, Drugs and Rock'n Roll

Jazz was losing adepts, coming to a dead end in 1960 with the "free jazz" of Ornette Coleman, Eric Dolphy and Cecil Taylor. Something to replace it was definitely needed. Given the demographic curve of the "baby boomers", the answer was obvious. What was needed was music by young people for young people. Even more so given the potential market that was out there, just waiting to grow bigger and bigger.

It all began in 1955 when Elvis Presley made his first recording and a film with a soundtrack by Bill Haley called "Rock Around the Clock" was released. The music was called Rock 'n Roll, but individual performances made for different sounds. There was Chuck Berry and his "Go, Johnny Go"; Fats Domino and "Blueberry Hill"; Little Richard and "Tutti Frutti"; Ray Charles and "What'd I Say"; Buddy Holly and "That'll Be the Day"; Ritchie Valens and "La Bamba"; Jerry Lee Lewis and "Great Balls of Fire"; Paul Anka and "Diana"; Eddie Cochran and "Three Steps to Heaven".

Rock 'n Roll and Rhythm and Blues influenced one another. The encounter with gospel and blues ended up in Rock 'n Soul. Wilson Pickett, Solomon Burke, Otis Redding, and James Brown, among others, eventually led to Soul music. Dipping into these multifarious sources, singers like Aretha Franklin created their own highly personal music. Marvin Gaye, with his "Can I Get A Witness" became the hero and herald of a new "sound", that of Tamla Motown, an incredibly successful recording company.

Meanwhile, escalation of the Vietnam War led American youth to protest more forcefully. Their anti-war sentiment was most aptly expressed by three leading singers: Joan Baez, Bob Dylan and Pete Seeger. The three of them joined voices to sing Dylan's "Blowin' In the Wind" at the Newport Festival, which drew an enthusiastic audience of over forty thousand. A hymn to freedom, "Blowin' In the Wind" became the rallying song for the anti-Vietnam movement. At the opposite end of the spectrum, a charming group of youngsters called The Beach Boys was conquering America with their "Surfin' USA".

But it was in England that a great new sound was making its way. The Beatles produced their first record (which Decca turned down!) called "Love Me Do, I Love You" in 1962. By 1963, Beatlemania was sweeping not only Great Britain but the United States as well. In 1964 the Beatles produced "A Hard Day's Night", and their songs took the top five places on the American hit parade!

The Rolling Stones formed their group in 1962. The following year, the Beatles gave them a helping hand to produce their first record, "Come On"; it was followed in 1965 by "I Can't Get No Satisfaction". During this time, Bob Dylan was recording Dylan, Peter, Paul and Mary were recording Peter, Paul and Mary, while Joan Baez was producing "Farewell, Angelina". But the whole world was passionately involved in the contest between the Beatles and the Rolling Stones. The Beatles reached the height of their fame in 1967 with "Seargent Pepper's Lonely Hearts Club Band", and disbanded not long thereafter. As for The Rolling Stones, they have continued their career with ups and downs.

The idea of "peace and love" had made serious inroads among American youth in 1963, whereas in Western Europe, youth responded first and foremost to rock pure and simple.

In France, Johnny Hallyday made his first appearance at the reknowned Olympia music hall in Paris in 1961. But the big hit of 1962 was the magazine Salut Les Copains ("Hi Buddies"). To celebrate its first anniversary, the magazine organized a celebration that drew one hundred and fifty thousand youths to the huge square at Nation, in Paris. The crowd went wild for Johnny and for "yé-yé" music. Two years later, fans idolized Johnny when he married Sylvie Vartan, a popular singer in her own right. It was probably one of the most famous weddings in the music world until

Milton Glaser

Poster slipped into a Bob Dylan record (Columbia), 1966.

125

Elvis Presley married Priscilla in Las Vegas in May 1967.

Great Britain continued to produce a steady stream of successful singers and groups. Among the most famous were Who and the Pink Floyds, Donovan with his "Catch the Wind", and the sublime Marianne Faithfull with her "As Tears Go By". Great Britain welcomed with open arms the brilliant Jimi Hendrick whose attempt at building a career was in the doldrums in the USA. He cut his first record, "Hey Joe" in London in 1967.

In the United States, there was a major shift in the music world. "Peace and Love" was moving off in a direction different from protest songs. The Mothers of Invention and the Doors caught the public's attention in 1965, while the Byrds gave a California twist to Bob Dylan's "Mr. Tambourine Man" and the Mamas and the Papas spinned off "California Dreaming".

Indeed, everything was shifting to the West coast, for California was where it was all happening. As we noted earlier, Timothy Leary, author of "The Psychedelic Experience", was the moving force behind the first love-in, held in San Francisco, where thirty thousand young people chanted the new anti-Vietnam slogan "Make Love, Not War", surrounded by the smells of haschich and incense. At the second love-in, held once again in San Francisco the following year, some four hundred and fifty thousand youths came together. It was so monumental a gathering that it startled the average American, and so newsworthy that Time magazine devoted its cover to the event. The hippy movement was born. From then on, psychedelic sound became the rage, with its theme of "turn on, tune in, drop out". In 1966, the Lovin' Spoonful with "Daydream", Frank Zappa's Mothers of Invention with "Freak Out", Simon and Garfunkel with "The Sound of Silence" and Sonny and Cher with "I Got You Babe", set the tone...or rather tones.

In Paris that year, the magazine Rock and Folk hit the newsstands. It was a direct ancestor of Britain's Oz and Frendy, and America's Creem and Rolling Stone. It was followed by Best and Le Saltimbanque ("The Showman").

May 1968 brought a salutary outburst, and Janis Joplin drummed out her sensational "Cheap Thrill", with jacket illustrations by Crumb. In 1969, Europe was agitated once again. In London, the Who gave their opera "Tommy", which Ken Russell brought to the screen in 1975. The Led Zeppelin were laying the foundations of hard rock.

In Paris, the first issue of Actuel came out on the newsstands, while in Canada, Leonard Cohen sang his poignant "Songs From A Room".

In the United States, the establishment moved in on the protest movement. The film industry put its finger in the pie with "Easy Rider" starring Dennis Hopper, "Alice's Restaurant" directed by Arthur Penn, starring Arlo Guthrie. The daring musical "Hair" opened on Broadway. Show business struck a big blow by organizing Woodstock, that drew an audience of four hundred thousand fans. The record industry gobbled it up. Recognizing they were on to a good thing, members of the industry organized a festival held on the Isle of Wight in Great Britain, and another in Alougies in Belgium. But the incredible magic of Woodstock was gone.

In 1970, the Velvet Underground in New York, Max's Kansas City and then in 1972 in London, David Bowie with Ziggy Stardust set the disenchanted and decadent tone of the music world. In 1970, Janis Joplin and Jimi Hendrix died of an overdose within two weeks of one another. They were followed on July 21, 1971, by Jim Morrison, the leader of The Doors. He died, ostensibly of a heart attack, in a Paris hotel room.

Protest became a thing of the past; it was time for consumerism. Sex, drugs and rock 'n roll were no longer a way of life, but merely consumer products.

Film makers were once again interested in music for youth. At the Avoriaz film festival in 1974, Brian De Palma walked off with first prize for his "Phatom of the Paradise"; in 1975, Jim Sharman shot "The Rocky Horror Picture Show" with Tim Curry cast in the role of the ambiguous Dr. Frank Furter and Susan Sarandon in her first role. These two cult films replaced "Easy Rider" in the imagination of youth.

The year 1977 marked a turning point. The King, Elvis Presley, died of a heart attack (or else an overdose of candy and medicine?) in Memphis. The music sung by the Bee Gees in "Saturday

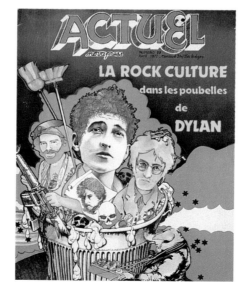

Benjamin Baltimore
Cover of Actuel, no. 19, April 1970.

127

James McMullan
Elvis Presley, New York Magazine, 1971. "Rock Is Loosing Touch With Its Origins".

Milton Glaser
Elvis Presley, poster and book cover, (Mc Graw-Hill), 1979.

Seymour Chwast
Elvis Presley.

Night Fever" with the dazzling performance of John Travolta led dancing millions from rock and pop to disco. Nothing was ever the same again. In France, singer Claude François was tremendously popular (he died in March 1978) and the first solo record made by Michael Jackson, "Don't Stop Till You Get Enough" was made in 1979. On December 8, 1980, John Lennon was murdered in New York in front of his apartment building, the Dakota, where "Rosemary's Baby" was filmed... Hard rock continued to have a following. In 1978 the Sex Pistols announced punk music. In Paris, launching platforms for new forms of music—reggae, African beat, Caribbean zouc and salsa latina— were La Main Bleue in the suburb of Montreuil and La Chapelle des Lombards in the heart of Paris. Peter Gabriel came here to do his "shopping" to prepare his music recipes for the world.

Starting in 1982 in New York, Grand Master Flash and "The Message" launched rap.

When all is said and done, the story of music during these two decades reflects that of minorities, struggles for autonomy and the right to be different. It also reflects the struggle between "me" and "we", that is, a fight between what is special about an individual and man's gregarious instinct.

In the mid-Seventies, Alan Vega and Suicide explored new paths and experimented with new sounds, just for the fun of it. The result was the magnificent "Sweetheart".

This exploration and experimentation led some twenty years later to a watered down form of music for the masses: techno music...

128

Paul Davis
The Rolling
Stones.
Actuel no. 1,
October 1970,
back cover.

Paul Davis
The Beatles.
Look, 1966.
On the
premiere
of their film
"Help".

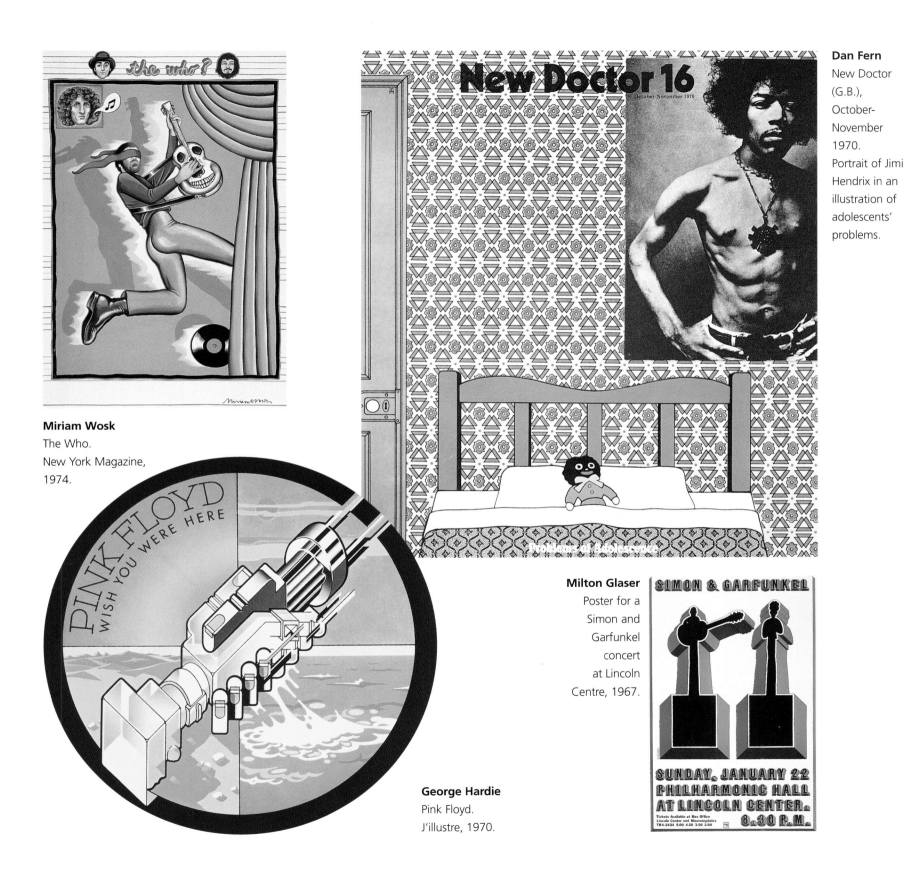

Miriam Wosk
The Who.
New York Magazine,
1974.

Dan Fern
New Doctor
(G.B.),
October-
November
1970.
Portrait of Jimi
Hendrix in an
illustration of
adolescents'
problems.

George Hardie
Pink Floyd.
J'illustre, 1970.

Milton Glaser
Poster for a
Simon and
Garfunkel
concert
at Lincoln
Centre, 1967.

Jean Lagarrigue
Esquire, June 1971.
"The Real Life
and Death of
Jim Morrison",
article by Bernard
Wolfe.

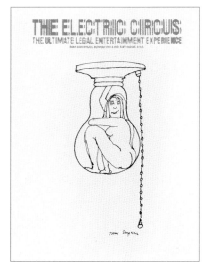

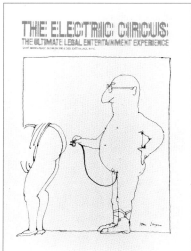

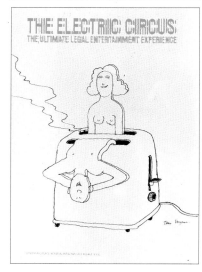

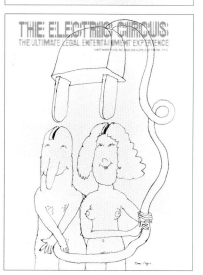

James McMullan
New York Magazine,
June 1976.
"Tribal Rites of the
New Saturday Night",
article by Nick Cohn.

Tomi Ungerer
A series of posters
for The Electric Circus,
the "in" place to go in
New York, 1969.

Paul Davis
"New York street scene", unpublished book cover design (Simon & Shuster), 1967.

The American Dream

How can one possibly choose from among America's abundant forms of culture and nature? What and whom should one choose? Seen from abroad, America can instill both fascination and repulsion, for it is not so much a land of contrasts as of quintessential extremes. Marilyn Monroe or Angela Davis? John Kennedy or Richard Nixon? (America's dream president assassinated in Dallas, but also the man who approved the ill-fated invasion of Cuba, who got the USA involved in Vietnam, and who was rumoured to have connections with the Mafia vs. the President who was forced to resign because of Watergate but who also disengaged the country from Vietnam and recognized China?) Henry Thoreau's ode to the land in "Walden" (1854) or Jack Kerouac's praise of the nomadic life in "On The Road"? "Gone With the Wind" or the striking "Punishment Park" by Robert Watkins (1971)? The FBI and the CIA or the Black Panthers and Red Power?

Paul Davis
"Montauk",
in Olivetti
appointment
book, 1974.

Impossible choices, but always an enduring dream. Everyone in the world dreams the American dream, starting with the Americans themselves. When Paul Davis did the illustrations for the Olivetti appointment book in 1974, he seemed to be vaunting the America of Paul Thoreau, but this did not prevent him from supporting activist minorities. In this, he fit into a tradition in American literature that perpetuates the myth of the Garden of Eden and of lost innocence with extraordinary lyricism and violence, and yet with curious reticence. Examples are legion: from William Faulkner to Jim Harrison, from Henry Miller to Thomas Pynchon, from Norman Mailer to Raymond Carver, from Francis Scott Fitzgerald to Richard Brautigan, from Olive Prouty to Sarah Schulman, and from Henry James to Malcolm Lowry. Theirs was much the same kind of opposition as between Thoreau and Kerouac. There are enough American dreams to go around, indeed to go around the world. On one hand, there's the elegant Fred Astaire and the athletic Gene Kelly, and on the other hand, Woodstock and "Hair". There's "The Godfather" and "West Side Story".....Nothing can surpass American films for nourishing the imagination and building dreams. Even small-budget films are spectacular and efficacious. Those who nourish the dreams of European film buffs are, advancing in close order, John Ford and "She Wore A Yellow Ribbon"; Samuel Fuller with "Big Red One"; Walt Disney and Tex Avery (not really in the same camp, appearances to the contrary); Gary Cooper and James Stewart on one hand, and Marlon Brando and James Dean on the other hand. One winner after another are Hitchcock, Walsh, Lang, Hawks, Capra, Lubitsch, Donen, Mankiewicz, Kazan, and Welles, not to mention the Kekas brothers and "Hallelujah the Hills" (1963); Nicholas Ray and "Johnny Guitar" (1951) and "Rebel Without A Cause" (1955); Charles Laughton and "The Night of the Hunter" (1955); Otto Preminger and "The Man With the Golden Arm" (1956); John Huston and "The Misfits" (1960); Jerry Lewis and "Mister Love" (1963); Robert Aldrich and "Kiss Me Deadly" (1955); John Cassavetes and "Shadows" (1960) and "Too Late Blues" (1961); Martin Scorsese and "Mean Streets" (1973).....Each in his own way adds colour, sometimes dark, sometimes acid, to the American dream.

In the art world, dreams were carried forward in other ways, with other images, abstract and expressionist with Rothko and Pollock, De Kooning and Kelly, or startlingly "realistic" with pop artists, from Rauschenberg to Johns and from Warhol to Rosenquist...

tion. Two of the most brilliant exponents of this new kind of journalism were typical examples of America's capability to move from one extreme to the other: the impeccable dandy Tom Wolfe and haggard, cynical, and biting Hunter S. Thompson. Wolfe's book "Radical Chic" brought him instant success, while Thompson gave us two books that were manifestoes: "Hell's Angels", which was infinitely more incisive than "On the Waterfront", and "Fear and Loathing in Las Vegas". Along with a few other writers, they contributed to two periodicals, The Village Voice and Rolling Stone, which changed the tone and even the type of the American dream.

As the "new values" of the young generation made adepts, the contents of the dream gradaully changed: handsome cowboys were replaced by "bikers", Boston gentry by Italian Americans from Brooklyn, the wide open spaces by an asphalt jungle, tuxedos by blue jeans, and "wasps" by minorities.

In the flood of impressions, music can claim an indispensable place. Woodstock, in 1969, was a turning point, for it gave pop music and rock a worldwide audience. But even before Woodstock, from the Apollo to the Village Gate, there was the inventive music of Charlie Parker and Miles Davis, John Coltrane and Thelonious Monk, with Archie Shepp and Ornette Coleman following.

In short, through her literature, films, painting and music, America was and continues to be the great dispenser of dreams, just as she used to stir up dreams of social justice and political reform. As far as the rest is concerned, Wall Street, Coca Cola, McDonald's and Heinz Ketchup incarnate an imperialist's dream better than any G.I. could do.

All of this is reported and relayed by what many consider to be the best press in the world. It was during the early Sixties that two editors-in-chief, Gay Talese of the New York Times and Jimmy Breslin at the Herald Tribune, invented the formula for "new journalism". They opened the door to subjectivity in American journalism and used techniques for news coverage which till then had been found only in fiction writing, such as dialogue, soliloquy and personal viewpoint. In a manner of speaking, it was a transposition in written form of what was already happening in editorialized illustra-

Even so, the dream still existed, even though it was fed by a continuing, triumphant form of schizophrenia.

Two films made in the late Seventies give a good idea of this all-pervasive ambiguity: in 1978, Michael Cimino directed "The Deer Hunter"; the following year came "Apocalypse Now" by Francis Ford Coppola. Needless to say, both dealt with the haunting subject of the Vietnam War. Moving at mad dash pace, the films are at once tender and violent, grandiloquent and sensitive. Both are stamped with a fading sense of patriotism, a shuffling off of old values and with indestructible hope.

Jean Lagarrigue
Lui, 1970.
"Un enfant du
Sentier qui n'a
pas mal tourné",
Portrait of Claude
Berri on the show-
ing of his film
"Le cinéma
de papa".

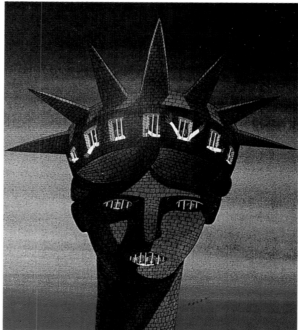

**Jean-Michel
Folon**
Cover of Time
Magazine, 1966.

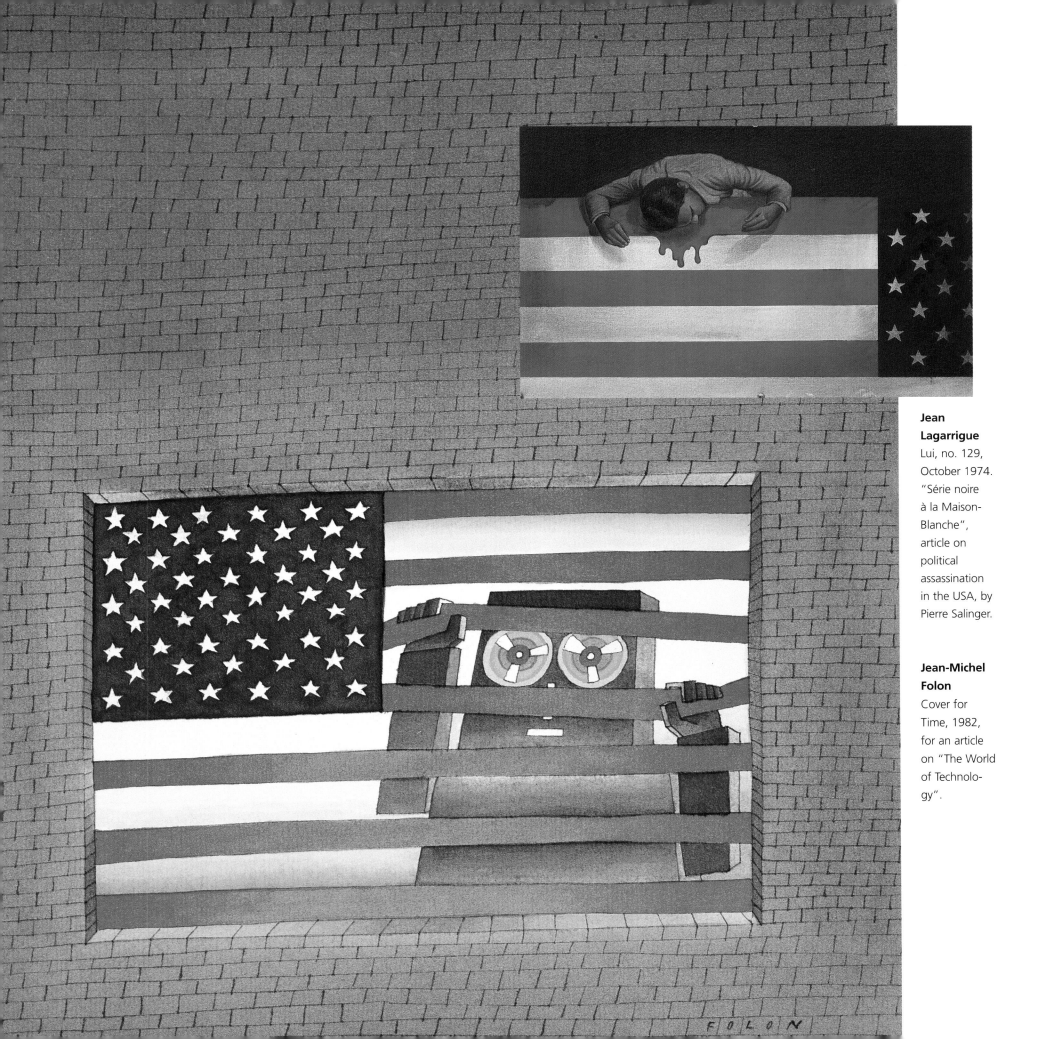

Jean Lagarrigue
Lui, no. 129, October 1974. "Série noire à la Maison-Blanche", article on political assassination in the USA, by Pierre Salinger.

Jean-Michel Folon
Cover for Time, 1982, for an article on "The World of Technology".

Tomi Ungerer
"Join the Free and Fat Society".
Poster, 1967.

144

Andresjz Dudzinski
The New Republic,
1981. "American
isolationism".

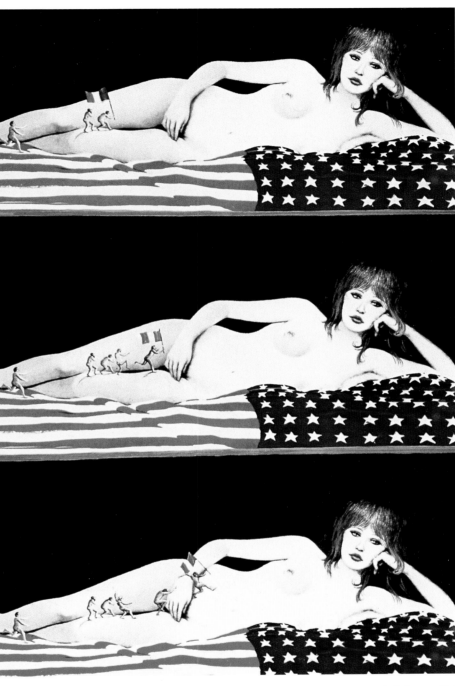

Gabriel Pascalini
Lui, 1966.
"The Conquest of America", an article
on the French who have gone
to the States and succeeded.

SOCIETY

145

Patrick Arlet
Playboy France,
1973. "New
York Graffiti".

**Andresjz
Dudzinski**
"The Dream of
America and
the Chrysler
Building", 1979.

**Gabriel
Pascalini**
"Utopian
Seduction",
unpublished,
1983.

147

Rear Windows
The French At the New Yorker

The New Yorker! A dream, an apotheosis, a legend... Everyone in the illustration business dreamed of working for the New Yorker, even more than they dreamed of America. There was no greater consecration that to do the cover of the most prestigious, the most quintessential magazine of the city of New York. Even today, in spite of major editorial changes to adapt the magazine to the demands of the times, the New Yorker continues to be a legend.

In the golden age of the New Yorker, every illustrator tried his luck and dreamed of landing a commission. But only a handful were finally chosen by Jim Geraghty, the art director, known for his tough but fair judgement.

Among the chosen few were three Frenchmen who together can take credit for one hundred and fifty covers. Spanning thirty years, André François, Pierre Le-Tan and Jean-Jacques Sempé delighted New Yorker readers.

André François got an early start as a book illustrator; in 1949, he published his first book called "Little Bob Brown". It won a number of prizes and started him off on a career as a children's book illustrator.

By the late Fifties, he had become well known in London and Paris as a cartoonist, an illustrator and poster designer. As his production grew, his reputation crossed the Atlantic. He was contacted by Frank Model, who was one of the illustrators at the New Yorker, to develop some form of collaboration. Things didn't work out, but a few years later, François met Jim Geraghty, who defined the philosophy of New Yorker covers in one short sentence: "I can't tell you what a New Yorker cover is supposed to look like, except that it's a drawing with the New Yorker printed above it. The rest is up to you."

The first cover illustration by André François dates back to 1963. Another sixty were to follow, each marked by the illustrator's special sense of humour. In each and every one, he depicted a window. Curiously enought, the same motif was also used by Le-Tan and Sempé. It was as if the New Yorker represented for them all an open window on the world, a world of intelligence and high quality.

The story of Pierre Le-Tan is somewhat different. In 1968, Le-Tan was still a high-school student. His parents had a subscription to the New Yorker. He himself loved to draw and was wildly enthusiastic about the magazine's covers. He had a grand time drawing some covers and, with the nerve that only a neophyte can muster up, he decided to mail them to Jim Geraghty, whose name he had seen in the magazine credits. Some drawings were sent back with a nice accompanying note, but others were kept for possible future publication. When his first cover appeared in 1970, Le-Tan was only nineteen. This was the first time one of his drawings was published! He left for New York, met Jim Geraghty and saw his dream come true.

Geraghty was born in New York of Irish parents. He was a somewhat churlish man, always dressed in tweeds, and extremely well versed in literature and the visual arts. Le-Tan stayed in New York for a few months. Geraghty invited him to join the magazine's illustrators and cartoonists at their weekly meetings, held every Tuesday. In the eyes of the young Frenchman, it seemed that all his colleagues lived in plush sections of Connecticut, were elegantly dressed and very glib. They reminded him of the characters created by Hopper and Leyendecker...

André François

149

André François

In 1973, Jim Geraghty left the New Yorker for other pastures. He was replaced as artistic director by Lee Lorenz, an in-house cartoonist, who carried on the house tradition for quality.

Le-Tan's collaboration with the New Yorker continued, and he eventually produced a total of twenty-five covers.

Jean-Jacques Sempé began his collaboration with the New Yorker in 1968. For most New Yorkers, he epitomized the French spirit. What is more, he had a wonderfully wistful sense of humour.

The New Yorker contacted Sempé, and in the spirit defined by Jim Geraghty to André François, the magazine gave the illustrator complete freedom of choice as far as subject matter and style were concerned.

The collaboration begun some twenty years ago still continues. The result has been more than sixty covers in which one recognizes Sempé's tremendous talent, his finesse and that bittersweet atmosphere that characterizes his work. André François, Pierre Le-Tan and Jean-Jacques Sempé make up a trio of unsurpassed talent. They represent the "French dream" for Americans.

Together, they have totalled nearly one hundred and fifty covers. As in a recurrent dream, there is often a mysterious window giving onto wide open spaces.

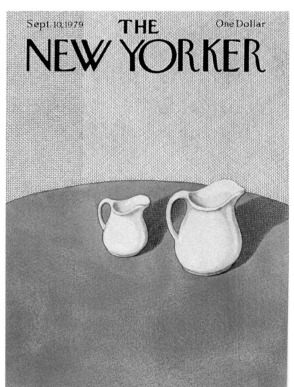

**Jean-Jacques
Sempé**

Jean-Jacques
Sempé

Campbell's
Campbell's
Campbell's
Campbell's
Campbell's
Campbell's
Campbell's
Campbell's
Campbell's
Campbell's
Campbell's
Campbell's
Campbell's
Campbell's

The Adventures of A Lovely "Lady"
Jean Lagarrigue and the Statue of Liberty

Ever since President Cleveland unveiled the "Lady" on October 28, 1886, millions have gazed at the Statue of Liberty from ships about to dock in New York. For immigrants to America, it is their first glimpse of the Promised Land…. a promised land that chose as its finest symbol the Statue of Liberty. The gift of France to its friend and ally across the Atlantic, this incarnation of "Liberty lighting the world" was the creation of sculptor Frédéric-Auguste Bartholdi; one of the greatest engineers of the time, Gustave Eiffel, designed the metal structure within. Is it any wonder that pictures of the statue set a young French boy dreaming? The boy's name was Jean Lagarrigue, and he was to become one of the leading illustrators and art directors of his generation.

When he graduated from the Ecole Nationale Supérieure des Arts Décoratifs, Lagarrigue left for New York to do a master's degree at the School of Visual Arts. His professors were none other than Milton Glaser, Henry Wolf and Robert Weaver. The first thing he did upon arrival was to head for Battery Park, where the ferry boats left, to meet the lady of his life. Having climbed to the platform behind the lady's crown, some three hundred feet from the ground, the young Frenchman gazed at the port of New York, ecstatic at the view of Manhattan, which looked like a sliver of glass and steel set between the East River and the Hudson River. He came to the conclusion that there could be no better symbol for America than this monstrously green, out of proportion, allegorical statue. The only possible competitor, he felt, might be Mount Rushmore with the heads of four American presidents blasted by dynamite out of the rock.

"Steinbeck and Co." Lui, no. 40, April 1967.

Jean Lagarrigue never really came down to earth after that first visit, and his initial fascination became almost obsessive. He started on a series of drawings of the statue, seen from every possible angle, as if he were doing a photographic coverage. The series was published by the short-lived monthly Twenty in 1962.

On returning to Paris, Jean Lagarrigue did the rounds of Paris publications to sell his drawings. This was a golden age for magazines. The men's magazine Lui was doing well, and Régis Pagnez had attracted such leading illustrators as Le Saux, Corentin, Castelli, Pascalini and Goude. Lagarrigue joined the group and worked at a furious pace.

Then, in 1967, the Statue of Liberty suddenly cropped up in his drawings once again. To illustrate an article on Steinberg for Lui, he used the shadow of the Statue of Liberty against a background of Campbell soup cans (see page 156). It was a twin homage to New York, via the Lady and Andy Warhol.

During the following months, he was busy doing illustrations for magazines and even some advertising, notably for Saint-Gobain and Camping Gaz. And there were winks at Angela Davis, at Little Odessa and at Watergate…. And another monumental drawing based on the film "Planet of the Apes"; it presented a striking vision of the Statue of Liberty rising up from the city of New York, petrified with fear.

In 1968, Lagarrigue returned to New York, where he spent two years as co-art director of Esquire magazine, alongside Jean-Paul Goude. One of the first illustrations he did for this glossy, glamorous periodical was that of golfers discovering the Statue of Liberty under the putting green.

"A l'Ouest, rien de nouveau", on America copying French wine bars. Lui, no. 182, March 1979.

"The Multina-
tional Plot",
article by
René-Victor
Pilhes in
Playboy France,
no. 32,
July 1976.

Back in Paris in 1971 but nostalgic for New York, Lagarrigue published a fan-magazine called "Les Aventures de Miss Liberty", paid for out of his own pocket, where he was finally able to express the full measure of his fascination. Printed on the press of Arte (the engraving shop and printing house for the Andrien Maeght art publications), it had a run-off of two thousand copies, but only three issues were printed. To this day, some twenty-five years later, faithful subscribers are still clamouring for more adventures of their favourite heroine. In 1977, one of Lagarrigue's friends (1), who was in charge of one area at the Georges Pompidou Centre in Paris, asked him to put together an exhibition on his favourite theme. It was called "The Adventures of Miss Liberty". Divided into two parts, the exhibition told the history of the Statue but also showed the representations, adaptations, and misappropriations of this image done by painters, sculptors, poster artists, illustrators, comic strip creators, political cartoonists and photographers. It was an immediate success: the press loved it, and the public had a grand time.

One of the drawing cards was the unusual setting specially made for the exhibition. The works were shown on or in wooden packing cases, which was an amusing way to remind people of the two hundred and fourteen crates it took to pack the various parts of the Statue of Liberty for its boat ride from France to New York harbour.

(1) Publisher's Note: Gilles de Bure

158

"New York,
Red Square".
Lui, no. 232,
May 1983.

"First Things First"
a funny article by
Fred Wershofsky
that lists what must
be urgently gotten
rid of: among
other things, life in
New York, which
Laguarrigue here
compares with
"Planet of
the Apes".
Esquire, 1968.

American rebel
Angela Davis.
Lui, no. 98,
March 1972.

At right:
Angela in prison
Lui, 1972.

"Ku Klux Klan:
merde in U.S.A.
KKK toujours KK".
Lui, no. 200,
September 1980.

162

Original lithograph to
celebrate the American
bicentennial, 1976.

"Immigration,
Even America
Says No",
Courrier
International,
August 19, 1993.

L'Express, 1979.
Article on the
devaluation of
the dollar.

At left:
"Dig", article by
Karl E. Meyer
on archeology.
Esquire,
February 1969.

"Miss Liberty
découverte".
"The Adventures
of Miss Liberty",
no. 3, 1971.

CŒUR DE CHIEN
MIKHAÏL BOULGAKOV
EDITIONS CHAMP LIBRE

168

New Look For Books
Alain Le Saux and Publishing

Lightning struck the closed circle of Parisian book publishing when a small new house called Champ Libre published "Coeur de Chien" ("The Heart of A Dog") by Mikhaël Bulgakov. As far as the literary quality of the book was concerned, there was obviously no problem. But the cover drawn by André François created a scandal among the purists of publishing. Much worse, most of the distributors were so shocked that they stopped selling it. The situation did not improve in the weeks to come. The covers of Champ Libre were enough to send a chill down one's spine. There were the covers by Corentin of "La Bande à Pierrot Le Fou", by Le Saux of "A Bas les Chefs" ("Down With Leaders"), by Reiser of "Le Rapport Secret de Khrouchtchev sur Staline au XXᵉ Congrès du Parti Communiste Soviétique" ("Khruschtchev's Secret Report on Stalin at the 20th Congress of the Soviet Communist Party") or by Topor of "L'Escargot Sur la Pente S'en Donnent à Coeur Joie" ("The Snail Merrily Sliding Done A Slope").

How this new company came to be founded goes a long way to explain why it shook the publishing world of the early Seventies. It is the story of the meeting of two young men, Gérard Lebovici and Gérard Guégan. Lebovici, thirty-six at the time, was a film producer and distributor. He was the founder of Artmedia and A.A.A. He knew everyone involved in the film business and was either loved and respected or hated. A strange person, Lebovici led multiple and sometimes secret lives. He was found

murdered in 1984 in an underground parking lot on the elegant Avenue Foch. The crime was never solved.

As for Gérard Guégan, he was a twenty-eight-year-old journalist who moved in the circle round the Filipacchi group. He was a regular contibutor to the Cahiers du Cinéma and from time to time to Lui. One of the best writers in the mainstream press, he nonetheless became one of the most rigorous theoreticians of the May 1968 movement.

Together, they decided to set up their own publishing house, and the choice of the name Champ Libre ("clear field") speaks for itself. They published, among other things, classic texts on Marxism and the revolution, subversive contemporary writings, forgotten foreign philosophers and theoreticians of situationism. The choice of authors was equally eclectic: Bulgakov and Clausewitz, Baltasar Gracian and William Burroughs.

Some of the books published in the early Seventies produced a shock effect, such as the correspondence of Groucho Marx or "Les Habits Neufs du Président Mao" ("President Mao's New Clothes") by China specialist Simon Leys. The latter was an up-to-date and forceful account of the Chinese Cultural Revolution. Up-to-date and forceful are the key words here. They also apply to the book covers, which generally conveyed an exceptionally violent message.

Others joined the pair in quick order. There was Floriana Lebovici, foreign literature teaching assistant Raphael Sorin, a militant Breton historian by the name of

Alain Le Saux

Small poster

for bookshops.

Jean-Yves Guyomard and Alain Le Saux. Le Saux acted at once as an illustrator and art director, and as such was the man behind the Champ Libre book covers. He brought together a merry band of illustrators, who were more familiar with the press than with publishing: André François, Topor, Corentin, Jean Lagarrigue, Castelli. He assigned two covers to Reiser, the first of which, "Free Jazz, Black Power", by Philippe Carles and Jean-Louis Comolli, remains a classic.

The books were produced under pressure, for they were as "hot" as a periodical. That is why they needed the stamp of a press publication, with covers that performed the same function as a Page One headline.
The team achieved its goal. Though distribution was poor because of blind prejudice in many instances, the books published by Champ Libre were easy to identity. This was even more important because the publishers

Reiser

Alain Le Saux

rapport secret de khrouchtchev sur staline au xxe congrès du p.c. soviétique

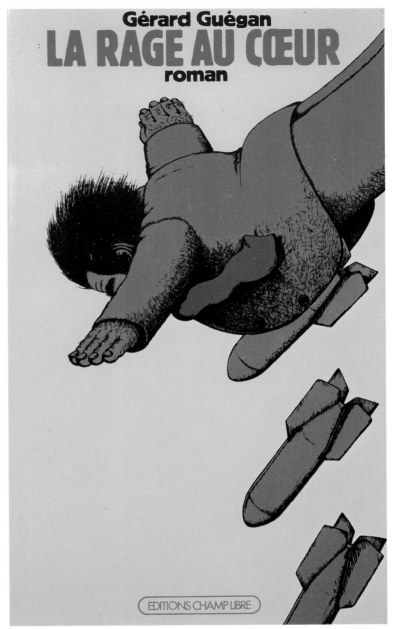

Gérard Guégan
LA RAGE AU CŒUR
roman

EDITIONS CHAMP LIBRE

had decided they would not send free copies to book reviewers. What is more, they refused for moral and aesthetic reasons to publish pocket-book editions. That meant that the first edition had to be sufficient to cover costs and to meet demand.

For four years, from 1969 to 1974, Champ Libre produced a crop of outstanding books with just as outstanding covers. In 1974, Lebovici decided to part with Guégan, Sorin,

Guyomard and Le Saux. The pretext was the refusal to publish Guégan's second book, "Les Irréguliers", even though the first, "La Rage Au Coeur", had been very successful. The real reason had to do with the review Les Cahiers du Futur, which the four took care of and which annoyed Lebovici. He detested the collection Chute Libre ("Free Fall") that published gory science fiction, of which two were by Farmer and another by Spinrad! It was a

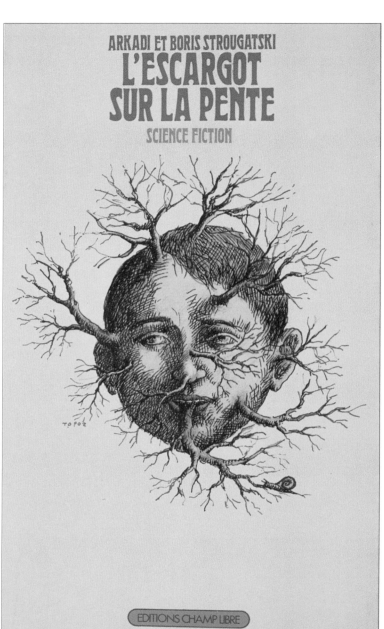

tremendous job, that initiated all sorts of innovations. It was Le Saux's private domain, and the three covers he did have left a lasting impression.

He handled each cover with brio, getting maximum graphic results with minimal means. The plastic innovations of Le Saux's covers give some idea of his curious combination of talents : a broad culture combined with extreme left aspirations, a taste for classicism and a passion for the avant-garde, coupled with an inordinate love of risk. He put all his talents to work for Champ Libre, the Cahiers du Futur, Chute Libre and, later, Sagittaire and above all for the review Subjectif.

Jean
Lagarrigue

Reiser

NORMAN SPINRAD
LE CHAOS FINAL

chute libre

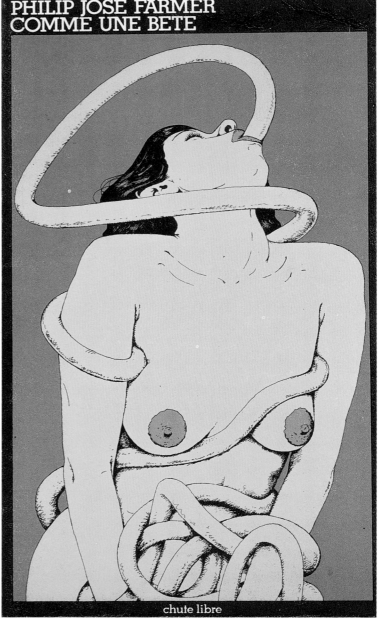

PHILIP JOSE FARMER
COMME UNE BETE

chute libre

174

Alain Le Saux

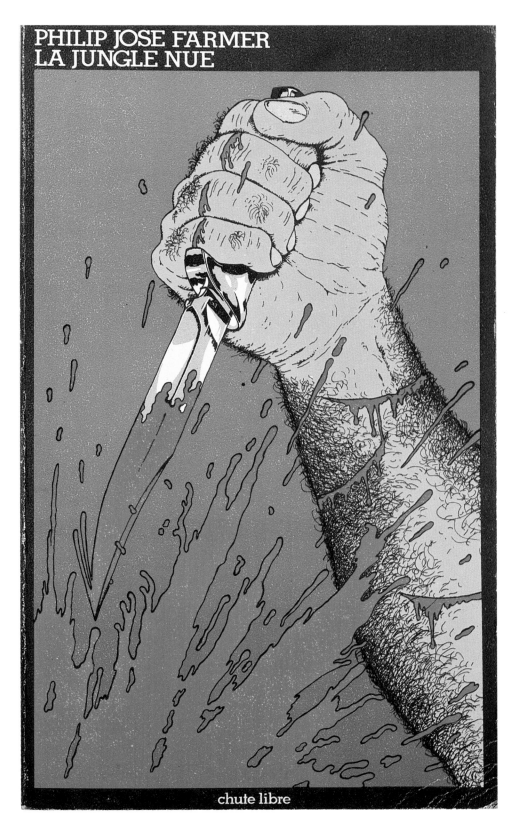

STREAMERS
BEST AMERICAN PLAY 1976
N.Y. DRAMA CRITICS AWARD

JOSEPH PAPP PRESENTS "STREAMERS" A NEW PLAY BY DAVID RABE DIRECTED BY MIKE NICHOLS
A NEW YORK SHAKESPEARE FESTIVAL / LONG WHARF THEATRE PRODUCTION
MITZI E. NEWHOUSE THEATER AT LINCOLN CENTER ———— EN 2-7616

The Spirit of the Play
Paul Davis and New York Theatre

Cooper Union Square, Lafayette Steet, downtown New York. It's six thirty in the evening, and the city is already sparkling with lights.

The lobby of the New York Publc Theatre founded by Joseph Papp is full of people. The theatre crowd is very colourful and variegated. There are people from uptown and from Brooklyn, from midtown and Harlem, from downtown and Queens. There are six different auditoriums that can be used for films or plays. The programs are excellent, well balanced, at once reassuring and innovative. Lined up along the walls of the main lobby are a series of posters done by Paul Davis at the request of Joe Papp. Among them are posters for "Streamers", "Ashes", "Alice In Concert" and "A Chorus Line", all of which were conceived specially for the Public Theatre.

There are also some posters commissioned by Joe Papp for the outdoor New York Shakespeare Festival, which he himself initiated. The series provides striking counterpoint to the other set of posters.

Over the years, the New York Shakespeake Festival has become just as famous an institution as the Lafayette Street complex. What a pleasure to go sit under the stars at the Delacorte Theatre, located in a corner of Central Park.

It was during the Seventies that Joe Papp founded the Public Theatre and set up the Shakespeare Festival. Imaginative, inventive, active and indeed indefatigable, Joe Papp was to New York and American theatre what a Jean Vilar with his Théâtre Populaire was to France, with a hint of Michel Guy, the founder of the Festival d'Automne in Paris.

A globe-trotter, Papp went from Latin America to Central Asia or even South Africa to explore new possibilities,

bringing back with him new finds in the way of authors, plays or ideas. In Poland, he discovered theatre posters that were simple, modern and hard-hitting. He was absolutely convinced that theatre should be for everyone and not just for the happy few. For the latter, theatre-going was easy, because they could afford it and had the cultural background necessary to appreciate it.

Papp loved taking risks and was in fact more interested in the theatrical "process" than in the finished product. And he was a stickler for quality throughout, so he took an interest in every component part: the script, the acting, the stage sets, the pace, the lighting, the comfort of the auditorium seats, the price of tickets, and quite naturally, public relations and, consequently, the beauty of the posters.

Thus, when he returned from a trip to Poland, he decided to try to produce the American equivalent of what he had seen there in the way of posters. He decided it would have to be a less cultural and more popular approach than what was normally used for "serious" theatrical productions.

That is what prompted him to look at magazines for inspiration. Flipping through the pages of Esquire and New York magazine, he found the illustrator who corresponded exactly to what he wanted, to the type of poster he hoped to produce. The style of Paul Davis was it: the imagery was at once very "early American" and yet the commitment was absolutely modern.

With Davis, Papp was able to develop an incredibly striking "language", that was perfectly straightforward and could be taken in at first glance. He wanted to create a strong, distinct identity for the New York Public Theatre,

"Henry V" 1976.
"Hamlet" 1976.
"Three Penny Opera" 1976.

as well as for the Shakespeare Festival that people would recognize. This induced him to pursue a steady collaboration with Paul David that was to last some fifteen years.

For those who criticized this approach by claiming that a great poster did not ensure box-office sales, Papp retorted : "Sure. But there will be a lot of people who will have seen the poster. Even if they don't come, they will have some idea of the play, which they can then talk about."

The commitment of these two men, Papp and Davis, thus gave rise to one of the most outstanding series of theatre posters that have ever been created. The series constituted a radical break from the classicism then prevailing in New York cultural events.

The close ups Davis did of Hamlet crying his suffering or the disquieting air of Mack the Knife in the "Three Penny Opera" are really more than posters; not only are they arresting portraits of each character, but they render the spirit in which each production was done.

Davis did another portrait-like poster for "For Coloured Girls Who Have Considered Suicide When the Rainbow is Enuf", using a very special treatment. The format is tall and narrow, and the face of the young black girl and the multicoloured letters of the title are set against a ground of white tile. It is a magnificent poster designed to grace the white-tiled walls of New York subway stations.

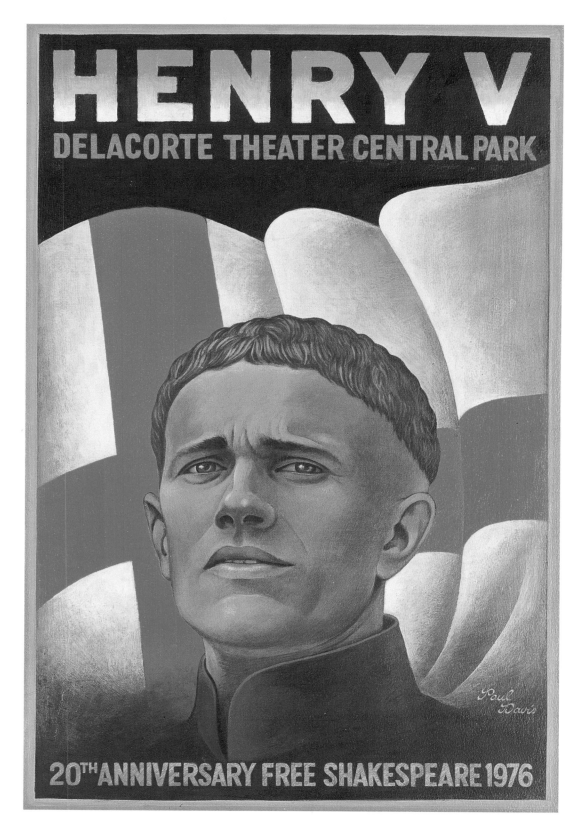

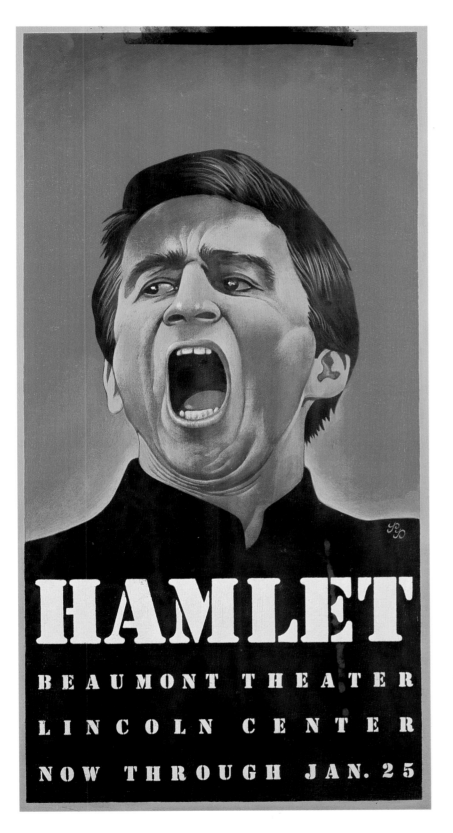

WITH MERYL STREEP AS ALICE
DIRECTED BY JOSEPH PAPP
CHOREOGRAPHY BY GRACIELA DANIELE
THE PUBLIC THEATER

"Alice In Concert"
1979.

"The Cherry Orchard"
1977.

"For Coloured Girls Who Have Considered Suicide When the Rainbow Is Enuf"
1977.

"The Pirates
of Penzance"
1980.

"A Chorus Line"
1980.

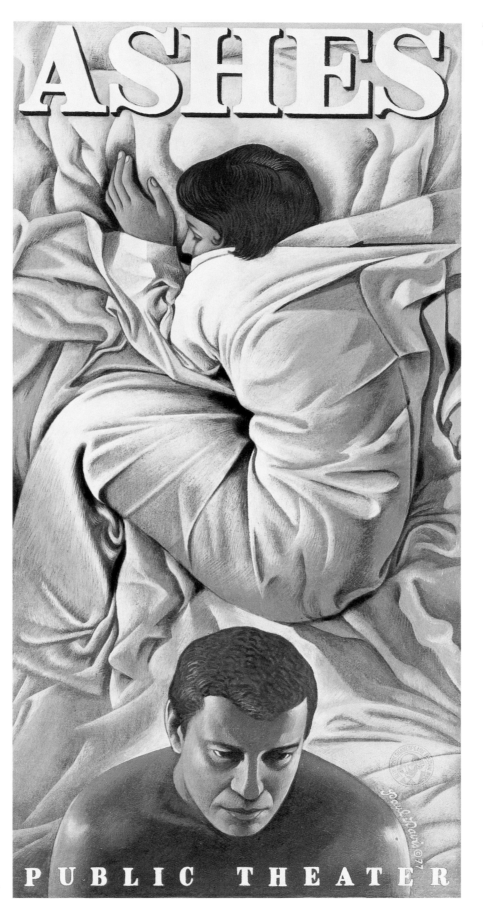

"Ashes"
1977.

Rock Dreams
Guy Peellaert and Music

It is difficult to classify Guy Peellaert , for he is too big to fit into just any convenient cubbyhole. The career of this Belgian, who lived and worked in Paris, followed a curious trajectory.... a trajectory heavily influenced by films and music.

Films were the source of inspiration for a number of frescoes and posters, including films by Robert Bresson, Martin Scorsese, Wim Wenders, Robert Altman and Francis Ford Coppola. In addition, he designed the credits for a well known television programme devoted to films called "Cinéma, Cinémas".

He also worked in the music world, designing record jackets for the Rolling Stones ("It's Only Rock 'n Roll") and David Bowie ("Diamond Dogs"); three of his paintings were turned into jackets for the last three records made by the incredible Astor Piazzola. Peellaert made his breakthrough in 1966, at a time when he thought he wanted to be a stage designer (which, in fact, he was for a while at the Brussels National Theatre). He published a provocative comic strip called "Les Aventures de Jodelle", whose heroine looked exactly like the French pop singer Sylvie Vartan. In 1968, he produced another one called "Pravda La Survireuse", who resembled another French pop singer, Françoise Hardy. Both albums got a lot of recognition and were hailed as outstanding examples of Pop Art.

In other words, Peellaert moved in such different areas as stage design, painting and comic strips. In the late Sixties, he worked on a variety show in Germany that was directed by Jean-Christophe Averty and starred the Bee Gees and Julie Driscoll. For him, it was another planet, and he felt the urge to use lightweight cameras to do short films on rock music (long before video clips became the fashion), for he was constantly listening to all sorts of rock. His dream never came true, so he painted his musical fantasies.

Begun in 1970, a series of one hundred and twenty-five paintings called "Rock Dreams" was finally published in book form in 1973, alongside texts by the most famous rock critic in Great Britain at that time, Nick Cohn.

The book was published first in Great Britain, and then in Germany, Holland, France and the United States. It was a tremendous success, selling well over one million copies. In a way, this was hardly surprising, given the fact that all the youth heroes of the day were in the book: the Beatles and the Stones, Jimi Hendrix and Janis Joplin, Elvis Presley and Ray Charles, Bob Dylan and the Jefferson Airplane, Fats Domino and Ike and Tina Turner, Bill Haley and Ray Orbison, Gene Vincent and Eddie Cochran, the Everly Brothers and Buddy Holly, Frankie Avalon and Phil Spector, Otis Redding and

GUY PEELLAERT - NIK COHN

BYE BYE, BYE BABY, BYE BYE

ROCK DREAMS

traduit de l'anglais par Philippe Paringaux

ALBIN MICHEL

Cover of the French edition "Bye bye, bye baby, bye bye", (Albin Michel) of "Rock Dreams". From left to right: Elvis Presley, John Lennon, Bob Dylan, Mick Jagger, David Bowie.

Diana Ross, Jethro Tull and Alice Cooper, Johnny Cash and Lou Reed…

As one flips through the pages of "Rock Dreams", the spirit of rock comes through, with its sense of melodrama, orgies, romance, adolescent enthusiasm and Hollywood myth. Through its pages, one can sense the nature, the specificity, the vision and gestures of each of the heroes that went to make this gigantic saga. Above all, one discovers the rich imagination of Guy Peellaert, nourished by American films with a special spotlight on murder mysteries like "Kiss Me Deadly" by Robert Aldrich, "Laura" by Otto Preminger and "The Maltese Falcon" by John Huston. Other nourishment came from photographers like Robert Frank, Wee Gee and William Klein during his New York period. When all is said and done, "Rock Dreams" is not so much a book or a series of paintings, or even the illustration of the musical fads and styles of a given period, as an expression of tremendous desire…

Peellaert's desire was to make films, to do panning shots, lighting effects, daring framing, atmospheric lighting, and fast-paced editing. Peellaert was someone who wanted to embrace everything, to reach dizzying heights by going to the depths of things, to show everything, and above all, to attain the heights of evocative expression.

His book brings together ten years of music and films, thatrepresented an unprecedented adventure, an adventure that also brought with it the demise of certain attitudes and major changes in behaviour.

"Chuck Berry"

"Adolescent Dreams"

"Wilson Pickett
and Solomon Burke"

"**Nothing
is real…**"
The Beatles.

"The Rolling Stones"

Double Page 46 x 27,5 = 53 x 31,7.

"Crosby, Stills, Nash & Young"

192

"Soul"

ACKNOWLEDGEMENTS

The author would like to thank all the artists in this book who kindly opened
their archives and loaned a number of original documents. To assist in this
undertaking, they delved into their own memory and generously gave
permission to publish their works:

Patrick Arlet, Avoine, Benjamin Baltimore, Liz Bijl, Jean-Claude Castelli,
Seymour Chwast, Roman Cieslewicz, François de Constantin, Philippe Corentin,
Paul Davis, Di Marco, Andrzej Dudzinski, Dan Fern, Guy Ferry,
Jean-Michel Folon, André François, Shigeo Fukuda, Milton Glaser,
Jean-Paul Goude, George Hardie, Bush Hollyhead, Hedda Johnson,
Jean Lagarrigue, Bob Lawrie, Alain Le Saux, Pierre Le-Tan, Mathe,
James McMullan, Barbara Nessim, Gabriel Pascalini,
Guy Peellaert, Michel Quarez, Reiser, J.-M. Ruffieux, Jean-Jacques Sempé,
Gilbert Shelton, Virginie Thévenet, Roland Topor, Tract, Tomi Ungerer,
Charlie White III, Willardsey, Miriam Wosk,
Peter Wyss, Tadanori Yokoo.

We would also like to thank all those who,
in one way or another, helped to complete this undertaking:

Patrick Arfi, Jean-François Bizot, Claudine Boni, Jacques Clément, Myrna Davis,
Thierry Defert, Jean Demachy, Diogenes Verlag AG, Michel Gillet,
Martine Gossieaux, Raphael Sorin.

The Great Image-Makers page 9

The Fight for Autonomy and Identity page 20

Spitalling Violence page 32

The Faces of Power page 44

Men On the Defensive page 72

Women On the March page 58

Revolving Couples page 84

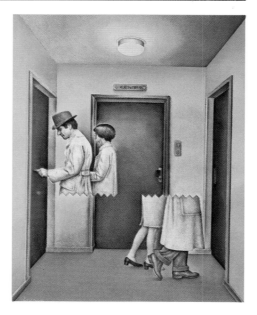

Combatting the World's Ills page 96

Existential Angst
page 110

Sex, Drugs and
Rock'n Roll
page 124

The American
Dream
page 136

Rear Windows
page 148

The Adventures
of A Lovely
"Lady"
page 156

New Look
for Books
page 168

Rock Dreams
page 184

The Spirit
of the Play
page 176